POETRY AND EXPERIENCE

POETRY AND EXPERIENCE

Herbert Read

HORIZON PRESS

© 1967 by Sir Herbert Read

Library of Congress Catalog Card Number: 67-13561

First American Edition 1967 published by

Horizon Press, 156 Fifth Avenue, New York, N.Y. 10010

Made in Great Britain

CONTENTS

NOTE

THREE of these essays, numbers 4, 5 and 6, are reprinted from my first book of criticism, *Reason and Romanticism*, 1926; they have long been out of print.

Of the other six essays number 3, *The Style of Criticism* has appeared in *English Studies Today* (Francke Verlag, Bern 1961), Lectures and Papers read at the Fourth Conference of the International Association of University Professors of English held at Lausanne, Berne, August 1959. Number 8, *The Resurrection of the Word* originally served as a preface to *Abraxas* by Arlene Zekowski and *The Multiple Modern Gods* by Stanley Berne (companion volumes published by George Wittenborn Inc., New York 1964).

The last essay, *American Bards and British Reviewers*, originally delivered as an Address to the National Poetry Festival, Washington DC in October 1962, was first printed in my *Selected Writings: Poetry and Prose* (Faber and Faber, London, and Horizon Press, New York 1963).

The Attributes of Criticism is a revision and extension of an essay first published in *Reason and Romanticism*. *The Faith of a Critic* and *Poetry and Experience* are printed here for the first time.

H. R.

Then I asked: 'does a firm perswasion that a thing is so, make it so?'

He replied: 'All poets believe that it does, and in ages of imagination this firm perswasion removed mountains; but many are not capable of a firm perswasion of anything.'

William Blake
The Marriage of Heaven and Hell

1

THE FAITH OF A CRITIC

In an essay with this same title published in 1957 I defined 'worthwhile criticism' in these words:

> At the basis is *pathos*. *Sympathy and empathy*— feeling *with* and feeling *into*—these are the essential psycho-physical processes without which all criticism is null and dull.

> It follows from this that there are no immediate [explicit] canons of criticism, no perfect critics. Criticism is good and sane when there is a meeting of [the author's] intention and [the critic's] appreciation. There is then an act of *recognition*, and any worthwhile criticism begins with that reaction.[1]

I went on to admit that 'recognition', a word given currency in criticism by Edmund Wilson (*The Shock of Recognition* is the title of a critical anthology he published in 1943), is inhibited by defects of sensibility in the critic—pathological limitations or psychological inhibitions. A critic may exploit his limitations and inhibitions, project his idiosyncrasies and 'tastes', and this seems to be the most popular kind of criticism (Mr. Wilson is an admirable example of it). At the other extreme is the scientific critic who maintains, in the words of Professor René

[1] Herbert Read, *The Tenth Muse. Essays in Criticism* London 1957 and New York 1958

9

Wellek (an admirable example of his kind) that 'criticism always demands analysis, explanation and substantial evaluation'.[1]

The ideal which I have tried to maintain throughout a lifetime devoted to the criticism of the visual arts as well as of literature is a combination of both methods. The basis of criticism is sympathy; the structure above this emotional ground-level is intellectual. Sympathy promotes understanding but it prevents judgement. Sometimes I have preferred to suspend judgement. I have often been accused of avoiding the 'substantial evaluation' of contemporary poets and painters. Is Eliot a greater poet than Yeats? Is Picasso a greater artist than (. . . Leonardo, Raphael, Rembrandt)? All these are questions repeatedly put to me and all are equally absurd. Is the rose more beautiful than the lily? Is Greta Garbo more beautiful than Marlene Dietrich? (I apologize for my distant stars)—to me all such questions are evidently absurd because I am asked to choose between incomparable entities. Analysis, explanation and substantial evaluation will only expose my own prejudices; as, indeed, they are exposed by the most would-be objective critics. René Wellek, for example, after deploring what he calls 'the random eclecticism of Coleridge's mind', admits that 'his very looseness and incoherence, the wide gaps between his theory and practice, his suggestiveness, his exploratory mind, his "enquiring spirit"—these will always appeal to certain apparently permanent

[1] René Wellek *A History of Modern Criticism* 1750-1950 Vol. II *The Romantic Age* Jonathan Cape, London and Yale University Press, New Haven 1955 p 82

features of the Anglo-Saxon tradition'.[1] But if a tradition has permanent features it must be for very good reasons—for reasons tested by time and experience, and in this sense such reasons are legitimate dogmas. Another tradition, say the Graeco-Roman or Classical tradition, may have equally permanent features, tested by time and experience, but I do not see how any critic can make a 'substantive evaluation' of these two traditions, in the sense of assessing their relative values (moral, social or aesthetic). We cannot, as critics, jump out of our skins—at least, we present a sorry spectacle if we attempt it.

I am not advocating a critical relativism, a permanent state of judicial indecision. I believe criticism to be a philosophical activity, concerned (to adopt appropriate words which Lord Acton applied to George Eliot's genius) with 'the latent background of conviction, discerning theory and habit, influences of thought and knowledge, of life and descent'. There are some words in this description that I would like to emphasize—for example, the *latent background* of conviction: not, therefore, dogmas aggressively exposed and insistently applied; *influences* of thought, not its inexorable logic, and influences, if I read the sentence rightly, of life and descent, that is to say, of heredity, environment and social experience. 'My life is spent', Acton wrote in the same letter, 'in endless striving to make out the inner point of view, the *raison d'être*, the secret of the fascination for powerful minds, of systems of religion and philosophy, and of politics, the offspring of the

[1] *Op. cit.* p 186

others, and one finds that the deepest historians know how to display their origin and their defects, *but do not know how to think or feel as men do who live in the grasp of the various systems.* And if they sometimes do, it is from a sort of sympathy with the one or the other, which creates partiality and exclusiveness and antipathies. Poets are no better.'[1]

Acton is describing what I would call a 'defect of sympathy'—or, to use a more exact neologism, of 'empathy'—in historians and poets whose aim is to be 'objective' or 'evaluative', and who fail because their minds are partial. In his own view (a view represented in our own time by another Catholic moralist, Gustave Thibon[2]) beliefs and morals are a habit of life, held unself-consciously, and a special faculty or 'sort of sympathy' is needed to understand them. That is why Acton held George Eliot in such high regard—she seemed to him capable 'not only of reading the diverse hearts of men, but of creeping into their skin, watching the world through their eyes, feeling their latent background of conviction, discerning theory and habit, influences of thought and knowledge, of life and descent, and having obtained this experience, recovering her independence, stripping off the borrowed shell, and exposing scientific-

[1] *Letters of Lord Acton to Mary Gladstone* London 1904 p 60-61 (my italics)
[2] Gustave Thibon *Destin de l'homme* Paris 1941 and *L'échelle de Jacob*, Paris 1946. cf. Acton: 'Good men and great men are *exvitermini*, aloof from the action of surroundings. But goodness generally appeared in unison with authority, sustained by environment, and rarely manifested the force and sufficiency of the isolated will and conscience.' From a letter to Mandell Creighton printed as an Appendix to *Historical Essays and Studies* London 1907 p 506

ally and indifferently the soul of a Vestal, a Crusader, a Nihilist, or a Cavalier without attraction, preference or caricature. And each of them would say she displayed him in his strength, that she gave rational form to motives he had imperfectly analysed, that she laid bare features in his character he had never realized'.

Acton and Thibon are only expressing a truth to be found in the ancient Chinese mystics, in Plato, in Spinoza, in Leopardi and in many contemporary psychologists: it is the truth that consciousness corrupts sensibility. Our decadence, aesthetic and moral, proceeds from such corruption. Just as the mystics affirm that all truth is a divine revelation, so the psychologist (or at least those who understand the creative process) affirm that the true work of art is impersonal: a form that emerges spontaneously from the mind of man, or rather, from memory, for creation is essentially re-creation, the recall of first impressions within a new ambience. The work of art is a thing *manifested*, as Wittgenstein has said; and though it takes its place in the world, the world of our experience and the artist's experience, it is not in itself active or activating. It becomes part of our ambience, along with birds and flowers, trees and stone-walls (and other people); but it remains inviolable, impersonal, unassimilable, something to contemplate but not to grasp. 'The attitude of looking and waiting is the attitude which corresponds with the beautiful. As long as one can go on conceiving, wishing, longing, the beautiful does not appear. That is why in all beauty we find contradiction, bitterness, and absence which are irreducible'—

Simone Weil's words, but let us not insist on the word 'beautiful', because already in Simone Weil's definition it incorporates contradiction, bitterness and absence, and it can embrace terror. If we become conscious of beauty it is no longer art; the work of art can be experienced only as a suspension of time and motion, as a still existence.

I do not resort to such gnomic terms to excuse myself an academic exercise; but I would excuse myself for the simple reason that I have never been compelled to practise criticism as an academic profession. My criticism is, fundamentally, a defence of my poetic practice, and that is the kind of criticism I most admire—the criticism of Milton, Dryden, Wordsworth, Coleridge and Shelley. Even within the profession there are welcome signs, after some thirty or forty years of academic industry, that the attempt to make criticism a science has failed. In what strikes me as quite the most impressive performance in this field, Professor Northrop Frye's *Anatomy of Criticism*,[1] there is a preliminary admission of nescience. 'The reading of literature should, like prayer in the Gospels, step out of the talking world of criticism into the private and secret presence of literature. Otherwise the reading will not be a genuine literary experience, but a mere reflection of critical conventions, memories, and prejudices. The presence of incommunicable experience in the centre of criticism will always keep criticism an art, as long as the critic recognizes that criticism comes out of it but cannot be built on it.'

[1] Northrop Frye *Anatomy of Criticsm* four essays, Princeton University Press 1957 p. 27

This is fair enough, and if, in the subsequent pages this critic's structures seem to be built on air rather than on artifacts, he returns in his last page to affirm, magnificently, that he envisages the criticism of the future as 'reforging the broken links between creation and knowledge, art and science, myth and concept'. It would be churlish to question the practicality of this Hephaestian task, but somewhere I have used another image that to my mind accords better with the irreconcilable elements: the laying of parallel rails that will, metaphorically speaking, bridge the distance between earth and heaven.

In this volume I have collected a few essays, some of them recent, some of them from the beginning of my published criticism, which are intended to show that throughout the years I have maintained the critical contentions with which I set out. My early essays were influenced by certain enthusiasms of the time—the 'classicism' of T. E. Hulme, whose posthumous works I had edited; the nearly related critical practice of T. S. Eliot, with whom I closely collaborated; and a few French critics whom we all read at the time—Remy de Gourmont, Jacques Maritain, Paul Valéry, Julien Benda. I have never made strong claims to consistency, which is an academic virtue, but I think I have been guided by what, in the preface to *The Philosophy of Modern Art*, I called a belief in 'the biological and teleological significance of the aesthetic activity in man'. This hypothesis has guided me in my criticism of literature no less than of the visual arts, and the pursuance of this aim has been consistent enough.

To repeat the claims I made in this preface of 1951:

> The method I adopt may be called philosophic because it is the affirmation of a value-judgement. To be precise: I believe that among the agents or instruments of human evolution, art is supremely important. I believe that the aesthetic faculty has been the means of man first acquiring, and then refining, consciousness. Form, the progressive organization of elements otherwise chaotic, is given in perception. It is present in all skills—skill is the instinct for form revealed in action. Beyond this physiological and instinctive level, any further progress in human evolution has always been dependent on a realization of formal values.[1]

It is possible that the function of form is not so evident in the art of literature as in the visual arts, but that is an illusion arising from the more acute 'semblance' (to use Susanne Langer's translation of the necessary German word *Schein*) of the visual arts. The distinction between the image in poetry and in sculpture or painting is a 'real' one in the material or physical sense, but aesthetically the function is the same: to serve as a bridge between those two realms for which we have many names—not only heaven and earth, but spirit and matter, essence and existence, the many and the one, the id and the ego, chaos and harmony, idea and icon. 'Among other unions of contraries found in beauty there is that of the instantaneous and the eternal,' Simone Weil

[1] Herbert Read *The Philosophy of Modern Art* Faber & Faber London, 1952 p 13. For a perceptive discussion of this philosophy of art, the best known to me, see *The Interpretation of Art* by Solomon Fishman, University of California Press 1963 pp 143-186

again. In this dialectical process there is no *permanent* synthesis except in the work of art. All spheres of knowledge, from mathematics to psycho-analysis, demonstrate this truth.

*   *   *

It may be that these fragmentary pages will fall under the eyes of some young student of literature as he contemplates the use he shall make of his intelligence in the years that lie before him. I would not ask him to take them as a model either of style or of method, but I would ask him to realize that he is being addressed by a man, once a student like himself, whose desire at his age was to be a poet and to serve the Muses in that great task to which all poets are called, which is not self-indulgence or self-expression but rather an intolerable struggle with the self itself, as an organism doomed to become self-conscious (and therefore word-conscious). A work of art, if he is lucky enough to create one, will be independent of the conscious self, a changeling of his imagination. He may disown it, and certainly his fellow men will not give him any credit for his assumed parentage. It is in such a mood of deception and disappointment that the poet turns to criticism. His criticism, as I have already said or implied, will inevitably be self-explanatory, self-justificatory, a mere pretence of scientific detachment. To the extent that his mind becomes philosophic he will, as Leopardi was perhaps the first to realize, cease to be a poet. The curse of our age, which we call civilized, is the preference it gives to philosophy in this sense—to self-analysis, to social adjustment, to knowledge as a systematic pursuit, distinct from innocence and wisdom. I do not think there is much help for you, young man; but in reading and judging these critical pages, it would be kind of you to remember that they are fragments from a conflict of this kind, and that what they lack in objectivity is evidence of a desire to preserve what Blake called an image of truth new born.

2

THE ATTRIBUTES OF CRITICISM

In the practice of criticism a writer will habitually isolate certain functions of his mind, giving definition and coherence to ideas that are invisibly related to other aspects of his complete individuality. If we adopt an image that has been more than once used of the mind, and compare it to a crystal of many facets, then we may say that the literary critic is accustomed to present only two or three facets to the light. The others recede into a shadowy perspective, or disappear altogether as to another hemisphere. Perhaps the complete crystal can only be revealed in a life developed fully in all its instincts and desires—a life, moreover, of active expression, demanding physique and will of an exceptional kind. Such a life, like Goethe's, seems to be admirable only in our theoretic moods: we have a more lively interest in personalities of an uneven grain, in which some faculties are developed at the expense of others, giving a sharp division of light and shade. These personalities (Rousseau, Stendhal, Nietzsche, Dostoevsky) have a greater effect on the development of thought because of this force of attraction. By their imperfection they appeal to our own faulty make-up and we can extend to them sympathy, pity and other humane feelings that represent in us the empire of fallible instincts. What is more classic and coherent leaves us unmoved, in an emotional sense, and is therefore less effective.

But whether the mind of the author to be criticised is of the integrated classic type, or of the fragmentary romantic type, it is necessary to begin with a concept of unity. The critic must aim to discover some utmost extent of mental territory to which the given expression of the author may be related. At the same time the critic should reveal the outer dimensions of his own territory. He must contrive to show all the main facets—those which reflect most light in his life. A spontaneous opinion or judgement is never uttered except as the offspring of a total attitude. It issues from the inner centre that governs and coordinates every reflection of the revolving spheroid. A literary judgement, though based on the closest scientific assessment of the objective facts, is not genuine unless guided by the subjective intentions of its originator. A view, not merely of literature, but of life is involved; not merely the science of writing, but also the philosophy of being.

To appreciate the flexible tendency of one's mind —to float with the current of one's likes and dislikes (and that is legitimate enough when the current flows steadily in one direction)—by such means a tolerable body of criticism may be evolved. But there comes a time when it is possible to see the vanity of one's own gesticulations, and then conscience cries Stop! Your particular opinions, given upon every or several occasions, tend to immerse you in their particularity. You have surveyed a long tract, measuring distances, taking angles, making notes: but you have not yet plotted out your map. Each essay is a collection of figures; your country is but a landscape travelled through: it remains to reduce it to an exact chart. Such an ambition may be vain, and in any case there is a dilemma involved. The past of any reasonable man is strewn with dead enthusiasms, and it is quite relevant to ask why one moment should be made more absolute than another. And there is an analogous fear that principles once enunciated may compromise the future. Once shaped out of the fluid consciousness, these personal ideas become rigid and irretrievable, exercising a suggestive power on all future faith, all aptitude for change with the changing times, all motives in a fresh conjunction of events.

These risks are nevertheless taken, firstly because one acts from impulse in such matters, and then because it is a possible fiction, to say the least of it, that one can in this way approach a condition of quasi-dogmatism. I hesitate to say dogmatism simply, because that would recall Dr. Johnson, who was anything but a scientific critic; and because there is some truth in Nietzsche's aphorism to the effect that the desire to find laws in nature is the mark of an inferior mind. But, arising out of any serious consideration of the discrete facts of literature, there are certain abstractions which have the aspect of universality, and I take it that it is the function of the critic to define these abstractions and by so doing establish a tradition which in some way or other is superior to the facts.

But, with these reservations, let us speak of dogmas, which are articles of faith. Faith is attained by a long process of experience, and without this rationale of experience, confessions of faith are difficult to make. They are not only difficult to express, because they demand clarity and concision if they are not to be abused, but they are also difficult to receive, representing as they do our most intransigent moods. Faith is aggressive, supercilious and often priggish: it arouses resentment because it is a standpoint reached, a certain definite attainment, beyond deviation or compromise.

The positing of dogmas—that is to say, *a priori* principles, whether concerning life or literature— is the only considerable business of criticism. Dogmas are the only solidities among successive and inconstant waves of appreciation and amorphous sensibility. The fear that dogmas infringe liberty should not deter us for a moment, for the final object of criticism is the criticism of dogma, and only those dogmas that express universal values will survive the assaults of the critical spirit. I mean the kind of necessary dogma that Nietzsche was concerned to establish in a book such as *Beyond Good and Evil*— what he called 'the moral imperative of nature'.

All this has been expressed more cogently by a philosopher of our own time, Karl Popper:

> Our propensity to look out for regularities, and to impose laws upon nature, leads to the psychological phenomenon of *dogmatic thinking* or, more generally, dogmatic behaviour: we expect regularities every- where and attempt to find them even where there are none; events which do not yield to these attempts we are inclined to treat as a kind of 'background noise'; and we stick to our expectations even when they are inadequate and we ought to accept defeat. This dog- matism is to some extent necessary. It is demanded by

a situation which can only be dealt with by forcing our conjectures upon the world. Moreover, this dogmatism allows us to approach a good theory in stages, by way of approximations: if we accept defeat too easily, we may prevent ourselves from finding that we were very nearly right.

It is clear that this *dogmatic attitude*, which makes us stick to our first impressions, is indicative of a strong belief; while a *critical attitude*, which is ready to modify its tenets, which admits doubt and demands tests, is indicative of a weaker belief. Now according to Hume's theory and to the popular theory, the strength of a belief should be a product of repetition; thus it should always grow with experience and always be greater in less primitive persons. But dogmatic thinking, an uncontrolled wish to impose regularities, a manifest pleasure in rites and in repetition as such, are characteristic of primitives and children; and increasing experience and maturity sometimes create an attitude of caution and criticism rather than of dogmatism.[1]

*   *   *

In an earlier version of this essay, written forty years ago, I proceeded at this point to analyse the basic assumptions of an American critic, Mr. Waldo Frank, who had recently published a vigorous onslaught on European culture (*Salvos* 1924) and in a prophetic vein had asserted the dawn of a new consciousness in America destined to replace our dying values. In the interval much has happened which would seem to justify Mr. Frank's predictions. Europe has suffered another devastating war and is still divided into irreconcilable camps which reflect

[1] Karl R. Popper *Conjectures and Refutations* Routledge & Kegan Paul, London 1963 p 49

the break-up of any intellectual unity that may at one time have prevailed. But can we say that there is any sign that our dying or disrupted values have been replaced by the emergent values of a new and vigorous American culture? The social economy that has been built up by the United States during Europe's agonized epoch is the envy of the rest of the world, and though it may still rest on an uneasy faith in the stability of the dollar (fundamentally an uneasy faith in the capitalist system itself) and though as a society the United States has social problems that are apparently insoluble (the racial problem, the unemployment problem) yet at the present moment as an economy the nation presents a monolithic uniformity that contrasts strikingly with the disunity of the rest of the western world. But does this monolithic uniformity invoke or inspire a culture of corresponding force and originality?

Perhaps the first question we should ask is whether the concept of a 'new' culture is in itself valid. The more one studies the phenomenon of culture the more one is made to realize its complexity, its interdependence, its ambiguity. In the words of a great archaeologist, 'we are confronted with concrete differences embraced within an abstract entity'.[1] The European tradition itself is an abstract entity and the concrete differences within it (classical, medieval, romantic—all again abstract entities which must be broken down into relatively concrete differences) are diverse enough to embrace any new phenomena that

[1] V. Gordon Childe 'A Prehistorian's Interpretation of Diffusion' *Independence, Convergence, and Borrowing* Harvard University Press 1937 p 17

may have appeared in the United States during the past half-century. This is demonstrably true of such movements as 'the New Criticism' in literature and 'Action Painting' in painting.

An American critic, Harold Rosenberg,[1] has called me a typical representative of 'the tradition of the new' and admittedly I have sometimes presented art as essentially a revolutionary activity. At the same time I have always insisted on the permanence or universality of the formal values—the abstract entities—of art. Art is consistently revolutionary because it is engaged all the time in breaking down rigid conventions of thought and character, in creating in their place the new symbols of immediacy and sensitive awareness ('concrete differences'). The difference between Bouguereau and Cézanne, or between Cézanne and Picasso, or between Picasso and de Kooning, is not an aesthetic difference; much less is it a national difference. The same 'laws' can be discerned in the work of all these artists. Any difference between them springs from the orientation of the artist's own sensibility, its scope and candour in relation to a social context. Criticism is the art of reconciling such contradictions.

Such contradictions have always existed within a cultural tradition—above all, within the complex tradition of European culture. Historically there is no discontinuity between the culture of the Middle Ages and the culture of the Renaissance. The same abstract entities continue to embrace the concrete differences of particular persons in particular places

[1] Harold Rosenberg *The Tradition of the New* Horizon Press, New York 1959

at particular times. It is possible to show that the opposition between even such seemingly abstract entities as Scholasticism and Empiricism corresponds to deep-rooted psychological orientations which from time to time alternate in their distribution or dominance.

It would take us too far from our immediate subject to explain this opposition in detail, but it is an opposition reflected in all forms of sensibility: in the opposition between natural and transcendental religions, between representational and non-representational art, between humanistic and absolute philosophies, between idealistic and realistic politics. The opposition is perhaps in the end to be traced to material and economic factors, such as the contact between the seeming friendliness of nature in a southern climate and the seeming aggressive terror of nature in a northern climate. It has its microcosmic aspect or analogue in the individual, particularly in the distinction between extraverted and introverted types, or, to be still more materialistic, between Sheldon's viscerotonic, somatotonic and cerebrotonic types.

The tradition of the northern European or Germanic races is, in its emotional aspects, the Gothic tradition—transcendental religion, non-representational art and a non-humanistic philosophy. Intellect, because of its logical, abstract and universal nature, is not subject to such a characterization; the emotions respond to environment, but the intellect evades it. The philosophy of Aristotle may owe some of its concreteness to its Aryan racial origins, but by reason of its abstract intellectual cast it was easily absorbed into the emotional attitude of the Gothic spirit: there was no conflict of mind and emotion, or rather, of two emotional attitudes. In this way scholasticism became the intellectual correlative of Gothic art, and this fusion of concrete differences and abstract entities had achieved its perfect unity by the beginning of the thirteenth century. Here was the foundation of what we call the Western European tradition; the Renaissance and all that followed, Humanists, Cartesians and the rest, were but concrete variations of that continuous tradition. All else is 'mannerism', even the so-called Classical Revival. Most of the manifestations of 'modernism' are mannerist in this sense. Only the style that begins with Cézanne and evolves through Cubism to Constructivism is 'classical' in the sense we use that word to describe styles that revert to the abstract entities of impersonalism and universality.

The failure of modern criticism to establish any general standards (such as Aristotle established for Greek drama in his *Poetics*) is a consequence of its surrender to a mannerist proliferation of styles—or rather, to its avoidance of the problem of style. Considering that ours has been 'an age of criticism' this may seem like a perverse and pessimistic conclusion. Indeed, Professor Stallman, to whom we are indebted for one of the best surveys of modern criticism,[1] claims that 'the structure of critical ideas and the practical criticism that British critics—Leavis, Turnell, Empson, Read—and American

[1] *Critiques and Essays in Criticism 1920-1948* Selected by Robert Wooster Stallman. The Ronald Press, New York 1949 p 506

critics—Ransom, Tate, Brooks, Warren, Blackmur, Winters—have contrived upon the foundations of Eliot and Richards, constitute an achievement in criticism the like of which has not been equalled in any previous period of our literary history'.

It would seem, since my own name is included in Professor Stallman's list, that I am about to condemn myself. It is true that I have occasionally indulged in 'the psychological approach' and that this, according to Professor Stallman, 'is actually leading us away from the fact of the art-work'. But Aristotle, too, indulged in the psychological approach (what else is his whole theory of catharsis?) and in practice there is no inconsistency between the psychological and its complementary approach, which we call formal. Form is a psychological fact. My whole critical purpose has been to show that form is an organic, indeed a biological phenomenon.[1] I have been in need of psychology to define form. In this I think I have been faithful to the two critics I have most admired in my time—Valéry and Eliot. Valéry's 'Form alone exists—only form preserves the works of the mind' and Eliot's 'Not our feelings but the pattern which we make of our feelings is the centre of value' —these have been the guiding principles of all my criticism, in the fine arts as well as in literature. But again I insist that 'the centre of value' cannot be reached without psychological tools.

What remains in our consideration of the purpose of criticism is a social rather than a critical problem —all that Eliot indicated by 'the loss of tradition'. I

[1] cf Herbert Read *Origins of Form in Art* Thames & Hudson, London 1965

am prepared to believe that as critics we shall never succeed in our aim so long as we lack some feeling for order in our society. But there has been even less agreement as to what constitutes 'order in society' than there has been as to what constitutes form in poetry, or style in any form of art. Eliot, like Yeats and perhaps even Valéry, longed for some authoritarian form of society. I have held that the only form of society in which our aesthetic values can assert themselves is libertarian or 'organic'. The structure of the right kind of society would be aesthetic—government, as Plato maintained in his *Politicus*, is an art, not a science. In such a hopeless belief I have been invidiously alone.

* * *

Hopelessness is the condition of the whole western world. We have carried criticism to the last degree of scepticism, even to the point where it becomes sceptical of itself, and have yet no new synthesis. We have destroyed our religion and have left the emotions without control. Emotions—which are individual, disparate, and therefore contradictory—must be disciplined in a social community. In former civilizations emotions have been controlled by religion. The function of religion has always been the absorption and unification of emotions—the real and essential identity of the Many in the One, of the concrete differences and the abstract entity.

That the critical spirit, expressed in reason, will ever evolve a synthesis capable of fulfilling the functions of religion is evidently impossible. Reason and emotion unite only in very rare and special perceptions; such perceptions are not capable of generalization. Emotions are too diffuse, too widely distributed, ever to be unified in reason, which is an evolved possession, never perfect at all, and only approaching perfection in rare individuals. But the negativeness of reason, in this sense, does not imply the reintegration of the old sacred concepts. The criticism of revealed religion has been operative not only on the empirical plane, which matters little, but also on the psychological plane. A religion like Christianity relies on the efficacy of unconscious symbols: it finds its most powerful forces in instinctive attitudes, like prayer, grace, and faith. The effect of scientific knowledge has been to destroy the unconsciousness of these symbols and attitudes: it understands them and therefore equates them with conscious equivalents, which are no longer symbols and which on that account no longer compel the imagination.

Waldo Frank, in the essay referred to, after an analysis of the culture of the western world that may be true so far as its goes, proceeded to an assumption that is wholly false. He argued that because the forces of intellect have destroyed our only unity, which was religious, therefore the *form* of our life is decomposing. This seems to imply an identity between the forms of life and of religious experience which is of doubtful validity. Religion is expressed in dogma; but intellect is a restless energy. It seems to me futile to say that because that energy has destroyed the dogmas, that therefore it has destroyed itself. It proceeds, rather, to the creation of new dogmas. But before the dogma comes the symbol; before the idea the icon; before the priest the artist.

The critical spirit has gained so much, after all these years, in clarity, precision, truth itself, that it is a pity to go back on it merely because it has left us, for the present, in such a naked condition of misery and chaos. We need to create a new unity, or perhaps to recover an old one. If the critical spirit cannot give us this, no other force will, for that spirit is the highest and most perfected function in man. *No other force will*: that is a large assumption, based on a faith in the consistent exercise of the human faculties of reason. But these are at the mercy of material chance, and what has not been achieved by the process of thought over many centuries may once again be brought about by a specific event—by the emergence of an individual capable of creating symbols that appeal freshly to the unconscious needs of the mind.

The critical spirit is not essentially negative or destructive; it can co-exist with the creative spirit, and indeed what is the meaning of this misused word 'creative' if it does not connote a discarding of the false as well as a discovery of the true? Art is not an invention *in vacuo*; it is rather a selection from chaos, a definition from the amorphous, a concretion within the 'terrible fluidity' of life. The critical spirit has broken down many false idols, inadequate dogmas and useless superstitions of age-long force; and such things are more easily destroyed than replaced, so that we are left for the moment a little destitute of comfort. But intelligence is a growing principle in humanity and an excellent carapace for tender hearts. It not only shelters the growth of the spirit, but trains it to unexpected fertility. All progress is a question of deliberate preparation: the building of foundations, the accumulation of knowledge, the careful cultivation of traditions and the embodiment of these in institutions. And always discipline and order, with utmost clarity of statement and honesty of thought.

It has been a common saying, since Pope first said it, that a little learning is a dangerous thing. But far more dangerous is the learning which, though not little, is limited. It is idle to think that any good can come of a specialization that is not linked to some wider ethos, itself the product of a versatile intelligence, or that is not subordinate to general wisdom. And this applies not only to the scientist whom we regard rather rashly as the only specialist, but equally to the critic and the poet. A general idea, whether it be a new image or a new hypothesis, invariably springs across two hitherto widely separated concepts: it is the electric spark that plays suddenly *before* contact is made between approaching poles of magnetism. Only a universal mind is likely to contain these pairs of opposites and for that single reason (and apart from the question of general wisdom) the universal mind alone is capable of 'creative' thought. It may be said that this is an impossible ideal: that the rare occurrence of a universal mind, as in Aristotle, Dante, Leibniz or Goethe, is the definite result of a *lusus naturae*—of chance, in fact. But the universal mind is not necessarily of this order, and universality is a quality possessed by all the rarer spirits of any age: it is a quality I would ascribe, not merely to Aristotle and Leibniz, but to Lucian, Diderot, and Ruskin, as well as to Emily Brontë and

Boris Pasternak. It does not mean the possession of all knowledge, or even, necessarily, of any knowledge at all. It does imply a capacity *to receive* all knowledge and events with equanimity and unprejudiced percipience; and to build up a positive attitude on this clear and serene perceptual basis.

This insistence on a positive attitude implies a consciousness of values: it implies a scale. The elucidation of the concept of value is mainly a psychological question, and one that still waits to be properly stated. I. A. Richards, in his *Principles of Literary Criticism*,[1] attempted to solve the question in purely realistic terms. Thus 'anything is valuable which will satisfy an appetency without involving the frustration of some equal or *more important* appetency. . . . Thus, morals become purely prudential, and ethical codes merely the expression of the most general scheme of expediency to which an individual or a race has attained'. The artist thus becomes an adept in the organization of his impulses, and in the adequate communication of this organization. 'His experiences, those at least which give value to his work, represent conciliations of impulses which in most minds are still confused, inter-trammelled, and conflicting. His work is the ordering of what in most minds is disordered.'

My own objection to this theory is that it leads to an ethic of expediency, whereas my experience tells me that an ethical code is an imaginative and perhaps an irrational vision of conduct. It is an immediate or direct apprehension by the intelligence,

[1] I. A. Richards *Principles of Literary Criticism* Routledge & Kegan Paul, London 1925

C

and not the work of the discursive reason—that is a distinction established by medieval philosophy. The *value* of a work of art, of a poem equally as of a painting, consists not merely in the progressive organization of the impulses for freedom and fullness of life (Mr. Richards' definition), but also of the open recognition of a moral sanction which is, in the old phraseology, *revealed* to the artist. This process of revelation will also one day, I think, submit to psychological explanation, and perhaps already the methods of psycho-analysis and the *Gestalt* theory of psychology could justify this claim for the direct apprehension of values. In any case an adequate criticism must account for 'duplicity' in art—for the presence, in every complete work of art, of both aesthetic and ethical values (but not judgements). It is a distinction between visualization and significance, and from this point of view one that has been well expressed by a French writer for whom I have always had a considerable, if discriminating, respect:

The Fine Arts aim at producing, by the object they make, joy or delight in the mind through the intuition of the senses: the object of painting, said Poussin, is delight. Such joy is not the joy of the simple act of knowing, the joy of possessing knowledge, of having truth. It is a joy overflowing from such an act, when the object upon which it is brought to bear is well proportioned to the mind.

Such joy, therefore, pre-supposes knowledge, and the more knowledge there is, the more things given to the mind, the greater will be the possibility of joy. For this reason art, as ordered to beauty, never stops—at all events when its objects permits it—at shapes or colours, or at sounds or words, considered in themselves and *as things* (they must be so considered to begin with, that is the first condition), but considers them *also* as making known something other than themselves, that is to say *as symbols*. And the thing symbolized can be in turn a symbol, and the more charged with symbolism the work of art (but spontaneous symbolism intuitively apprehended, not hieroglyphic symbolism), the more immense, the richer and the higher will be the possibility of joy and beauty. The beauty of a picture or a statue is thus incomparably richer than the beauty of a carpet, a Venetian glass, or an amphora.[1]

M. Maritain is here mainly concerned with the art of painting, but his distinction is equally applicable to the art of writing, and there is no more to say on the matter. Poetry, in short, is delectation, and this delectation is something that surpasses joy in the music of words or delight in images, for words and images reverberate according to the quality of our knowledge, and the greater our knowledge, the more surcharged it is with the perception of values, the deeper will be the delight aroused in us. Art thus only gives joy in proportion to the understanding we bring to it, and our understanding must be of the most universal and intuitive kind.[2]

* * *

Finally, there is the dilemma usually posed under the simple terms of *head* and *heart*, but really involv-

[1] Jacques Maritain *Art and Scholasticism* translated by J. F. Scanlan. Sheed & Ward, London 1930 p 57

[2] 'Die Welt hat sich realiter zum Menschen emporgebildet, der Mensch soll es idealiter zur Welt'. Max Scheler *Die Formen des Wissens und die Bildung* Bonn 1925 p 12

ing a very complex and subtle psychological problem. In stating this problem we must try to keep to definite terms. A scientific critic would naturally, in the course of his practice, cite reason as a final criterion. Reason is a very difficult word to use without confusion. It is often used as a synonym for rationality, or even for a mechanistic logic. Reason should rather connote the widest evidence of the senses, and of all processes and instincts developed in the long history of man. It is the sum total of awareness, ordained and ordered to some specific end or object of attention. But obviously this element of order implies duration—it is a system constructed in time and operating in time. It seems needless, on the other hand, to deny the validity of that instantaneous type of judgement which we call intuition (*Apriorieinsicht*). In action, when instincts (or habitual reactions) are rapidly roused under the stress of danger or some other emotion, the mind can act without consciousness of its rational background; and act with precision and perfect rightness. I must not be led, at this point, into a discussion of the nature of instinctive judgements: I will only state, as my personal belief, that the *quality* of such judgements is determined by the previous rational training and equipment of the subject acting—in so far as such judgements are of more than immediate value to the consciousness. The majority of them are mere animalistic impulses.

But to return to the practice of criticism. There is in such a ratiocinative process little opportunity for the exercise of intuition. But people will be found to defend, under the shelter of this vague faculty, an emotional attitude that is not without its value. Literature is, after all, mainly an expression of emotional states. I would say it is mainly the control of them. But emotion is the original substance of all aesthetic forms, for even intellectual forms cannot have value as art until they have been emotionally apprehended.

The danger is that the critical faculty, elaborating its laws too far from its immediate object, may construct categories or ideals that are in the nature of impassive moulds. The critic then returns to the plastic substance of art and in a moment, in the name of science, he has presented us with a rigid shape which he would persuade us is the living reality. But obviously it is dead; it no longer pulses with that life and variability which we ascribe to emotional experience.

To guard against this false method, the critic has to maintain an attitude which we must describe in another metaphor. He is the man who has carefully elaborated a few dogmas, in the sure belief that without such fixed points no course can be steered, no height measured and no distances maintained. But having fixed his points, he does not stand still; he is impelled in some direction and the force that drives him is feeling or emotion. That is the final test of criticism: that its methods are perfected in science, but that its motives are spontaneous, impulsive—aspects of courage, constancy and devotion. The courageous act is instantaneous and the course of history is directed not so much by foresight as by insight, not so much by statesmen and philosophers as by scientists and poets.

3

THE STYLE OF CRITICISM

Two present tendencies of literature in the Western world may perhaps be accepted as self-evident: a development of scientific method in criticism without parallel in our history, and, perhaps also without parallel, a sense of frustration in our younger writers.

Criticism is very much alive; poetry, like God in Nietzsche's announcement, is dead. It will be my purpose in this essay to consider whether there may possibly be some causal connection between these two phenomena. Literary criticism has acquired 'principles' which qualify it as an academic discipline, and education has become so universal that very few potential writers now escape academic instruction. These are the new features of our cultural situation.

I have called this essay 'the style of criticism' because I believe that style is the best index to the purpose or intention of the critic. In the dissection of truth a graceless movement is as ineffective as a blunt instrument. Style has this double meaning of anatomy and grace: it belongs to a family of words among which we find such curious relatives as stickleback and tiger, instinct and stimulate, but common to them all is the sense, whether metaphoric or real, of something with a sharp point, and the Latin *stilus*, from which our word is directly derived, was a sharp-pointed instrument originally intended for writing on wax. Since writing of this kind was a skill, a manual craft, there developed from very early times a comparative sense of effectiveness and order which gave to writing the dignity of an art, and at first the art was inseparable from the physical activity of handling a pen or brush. It remains so in Oriental calligraphy. In the West, however, the form soon became separated from the content, though a certain ambiguity may have remained until the invention of printing. Writing is still a physical activity, and a psychology of writing, to be complete, ought to investigate the intimate connection that undoubtedly exists between the physical activity and the verbal style. We are all aware of the change that comes to a writer's style when he abandons writing for dictation, and even the typewriter has had an influence on style. 'Writer' is still a word for one kind of artist: the typist is a drudge.

These, however, are not the questions I propose to discuss now. I am to be much more concerned with style as a mental and indeed a moral discipline, as an index to what Whitehead called 'the ultimate morality of mind';[1] concerned, too, with the consequences, for education and creative literature, of the

---

[1] 'An interest, or taste, a category of scholarship, a poetic sensibility become disciplined in so far as they produce the peculiarly intellectual virtues, in so far as they lead to "the ultimate morality of mind", which significantly enough, Whitehead defined as "style". Sensibility, the intellect, the moral sense develop as a single existence.' William Walsh *The Use of Imagination* Chatto & Windus, London 1959 p 101

gradual abandonment of a stylistic criterion in academic criticism.

Buffon's famous statement, *le style est l'homme même*, is generally misquoted. In its context it is not to be understood as an assertion that style is an expression of the author's personality, but rather that style is a universal quality which if achieved will guarantee the survival of the author's personality. An alternative to the word 'style' is the word 'manner', and style in writing, according to the view generally held in the eighteenth century, was good manners in writing. But good manners, it may be supposed, always allow for some variation appropriate to the occasion and even to the social status of the man possessing them. Thus the way was left open for a distinction between a good style and a characteristic style—between a style conforming to impersonal standards of euphony and rhythm, and a style that is expressive of an individual temperament.[1] A theory of style then gets caught up in a theory of temperaments and from the time of Johnson onwards there was an indulgence of idiosyncrasies which Coleridge was to correct with his ideal of simplicity and his test of untranslateability—

> Style is nothing else but the art of conveying the meaning appropriately and with perspicuity, whatever that meaning may be, and one criterion of style is that it should not be translateable without injury to the meaning.

[1] The concept of 'Literature as a Revelation of Personality' is the subject of an illuminating chapter in M. H. Abrams *The Mirror and the Lamp* New York 1953 pp 226 to 262

Characteristically he ascribed the decline of style in the eighteenth century to the Revolution:

> The nation became much more commercial than it had been before; a learned body, or clerisy, as such, gradually disappeared, and literature in general began to be addressed to the common miscellaneous public. The public had become accustomed to, and required, a strong stimulus; and to meet the requisitions of the public taste, a style was produced which by combining triteness of thought with singularity and excess of manner of expression, was calculated at once to soothe ignorance and to flatter vanity.[1]

It is not difficult, on this line of argument, to find a social explanation for the disappearance, in our own time, of the very concept of style. Criticism is no longer addressed, either to a clerisy or to the common miscellaneous public: it is addressed to other critics and is calculated to exhibit learning and impress colleagues.

It is not my intention to discuss either the nature of style in literature or its historical development in England. I assume its desirability and I accept Coleridge's definition of it (which he stole from Swift) as 'proper words in their proper places'. But what we have witnessed in our time, that is to say, in the past fifty years, is a total rejection of style as a criterion of literature and a scornful refusal to observe its requirements in the course of criticism. Let me give you the evidence. Here, embedded in a work that has been justly received as an almost Aristotelian codification of the modern critic's methods, *The Anatomy*

[1] *Miscellaneous Criticism* ed. T. M. Raysor, Constable, London 1936 p 220

of Criticism by Professor Northrop Frye, you have the heresy nakedly exposed.

> The conception of style is based on the fact that every writer has his own rhythm, as distinctive as his handwriting, and his own imagery, ranging from a preference for certain vowels and consonants to a pre-occupation with two or three archetypes. Style exists in all literature, of course, but may be seen at its purest in thematic prose: in fact, it is the chief literary term applied to works of prose generally classified as non-literary. Style had its great period in late Victorian times, when the primary connection between writing and personality was a fundamental principle of criticism.[1]

The idiosyncratic theory of style is, it will be seen, accepted without question; and since we no longer live in late Victorian times but in the new scientific age, the whole concept of style is dismissed as an anachronism. Presumably Professor Frye would agree that some words are more appropriate than others and that their arrangement in a sentence calls for a special skill. Elsewhere in his book he draws a distinction, which throws further light on his meaning, between the artist and the ego in the artist, the latter being a will-o'-the-wisp who turns the artist away from his proper work to go and chase other seductive marshlights:

> The pursuit of beauty is much more dangerous nonsense than the pursuit of truth or goodness, because it affords a stronger temptation to the ego. Beauty, like truth or goodness, is a quality that may in one

[1] Northrop Frye *Anatomy of Criticism* Princeton University Press 1957 p 268

sense be predicated of all great art, but the deliberate attempt to beautify can, in itself, only weaken the creative energy . . . Whenever the word beauty means loveliness or attractiveness, as it is bound to do whenever it is made the intention of art, it becomes reactionary: it tries to restrict either what the artist may choose for a subject or the method in which he may choose to treat it, and it marshals all the forces of prudery to keep him from expanding his vision beyond an arid and uninspired pseudo-classicism. Ruskin spoiled many of his finest critical insights with this fallacy; Tennyson often hampered the vigour of his poetry by it, and in some of the lesser beauticians of the same period we can see clearly what the neurotic compulsion to beautify everything leads to. It leads to an exaggerated cult of style, a technique of making everything in a work of art, even a drama, sound all alike, and like the author, and like the author at his most impressive. Here the vanity of the ego has replaced the honest pride of the craftsman.[1]

It is easy enough to take the point of this criticism of style, but one begins to suspect that such a distrust of the ego is the sign of another neurotic compulsion, the compulsion to uniformity. There are sufficient assumptions and assertions in Professor Frye's argument to justify a counter-argument, and one that is not necessarily based on a defence of beauty. What Professor Frye is attacking, and what I propose to defend, is what he calls 'the aesthetic view of the work of art as an object of contemplation'. It seems to me that an aesthetic view of literature is compatible with any of the four types of criticism described by Professor Frye—historical, ethical, arche-

[1] *ibid* pp 114-115

typal and rhetorical criticism. For if the theory of style which I am going to defend is true, then it is true for all types of literature, including criticism. It is an assertion that style is that element in literature without which there is no art; and that to indulge in ethical or psychological criticism is irrelevant unless the stylistic criterion has first been established and is constantly applied.

Let us first consider the analogy of another art, that of painting, in which this problem has been considered for many years, and in which, outside the dogmatic and sterile doctrine of socialist-realism, an almost universal agreement exists among critics.[1] Since the publication of Riegl's *Spätrömische Kunstindustrie* in 1901, if not since the publication of Kant's *Critique of Judgement*, it has not been possible to conceive the plastic arts as other than essentially the expression of a will to form, and as being effective as external symbols of internal feelings primarily in virtue of their formal qualities. This formalist aesthetic may from time to time have been challenged in the name of idealism, in which the form is identified with the embodied idea; or in the name of sensualism, in which the form is not distinguished from the pleasurable nature of the response it evokes; but neither idealism nor sensualism altogether dispenses with the concept of form. To trace the development of formalistic criticism in the visual arts is not necessary for my present purpose, simply because I can assume that any other kind of criticism is not seriously entertained. It is true that in these

[1] cf. Meyer Shapiro, 'Style', in A. Kroeber ed., *Anthropology Today* University of Chicago Press 1953

arts too, we have historical, ethical, archetypal and rhetorical types of criticism, but they all, to the best of my knowledge, assume that the purpose of a work of art is fulfilled by its form. A work of art, as Panofsky has said, always demands to be experienced aesthetically and he defines this experience in the following simple way:

> When a man looks at a tree from the point of view of a carpenter, he will associate it with the various uses to which he might put the wood; and when he looks at it from the point of view of an ornithologist he will associate it with the birds that might nest in it. When a man at a horse race watches the animal on which he has put his money, he will associate its performance with his desire that it may win. Only he who simply and wholly abandons himself to the object of his perception will experience it aesthetically.[1]

The work of art, that is to say, is an object made with the *intention* of being experienced aesthetically. That is what Riegl meant by the *Kunstwollen*. A work of art is only to be distinguished from other modes of communication by this intention. The intention is rarely pure: the artist is human like the rest of us and may use his work to convey a piece of information or transmit a concept. The idealist usually asumes that 'the more the proportion of emphasis on "idea" and "form" approaches a state of equilibrium, the more eloquently will the work reveal what is called "content" '. But the formalist will insist that the form *is* the idea—that when a painter or sculptor conceives a work of art, he is using a mode of

[1] Erwin Panofsky *Meaning in the Visual Arts* New York 1955 pp 13-14.

thought; his activity is, as Conrad Fiedler was the
first to maintain, a mode of visual cognition. Fiedler
would say the same of the poet's activity—namely
that its primary purpose is not to convey information, which can be done adequately in prose, but that
it also is a mode of thought, a direct apprehension,
by means of image and metaphor, of the nature of
reality. There is a similar conception of the poem in
Hölderlin and in Heidegger's commentary on Hölderlin.[1] It is for this reason that a poet is emancipated
from the conventional rules of syntax.

I have apparently, but quite unintentionally, com-
mitted what is known to modern criticism as the intentional fallacy, but let me hasten to make clear that
when I speak of the artist's or poet's intentions, I am
not for a moment suggesting that this is relevant to
the appreciation or the criticism of his style. A writer
may model his style on the Authorized Version or
on Milton, just as a painter may model his style on
Michelangelo or Cézanne; but we judge the result
and not the process. The only intention that need
concern us is the intention of the artist to accommo-
date his means of expression to what he wishes to
express.

A consideration of the visual arts reveals that, as
Fiedler says, 'in the artist's mind a peculiar consciousness of the world is in process of development',
and this consciousness, peculiar in its clarity and
originality, is achieved by an immense, even heroic,
effort to grasp the world of appearances, to reduce it

[1] cf. 'Hölderlin and the Essence of Poetry' in *Existence and
Being* Vision Press, London 1949. 'Poetry is the establishing
of being by means of the word' p 304

to concreteness and exact focus. It is this individual effort of consciousness that constitutes the artistic activity, and works of art are, as it were, a by-product of this *Kunstwollen*, this desire to obtain 'a complete necessary existence'. This is a force of nature, a biological impulse, which has nothing whatsoever to do with the expression of ideas or the communication of social values—what Professor Frye calls, in an emotional lapse, 'the vision of the recreation of man'. On the contrary, what excites artistic activity, inspires the will to create, is, in Fiedler's words, 'that which is as yet untouched by the human mind' and he adds:

> Art creates the form for that which does not yet in any way exist for the human mind and for which it contrives to create forms on behalf of the human mind. Art does not start from abstract thought in order to arrive at forms; rather, it climbs up from the formless to the formed, and in this process is found its entire mental meaning.[1]

Art is always, whether visual, verbal or aural, such a process of formation, a crystallization of the amorphous nature of our human existence, and that *process* is the style of art: style is the grace and clarity with which that activity is performed. Malraux in *The Voices of Silence* has a similar if less precise definition:

> Every true style is a scaling-down to our human perspective of that eternal flux on whose mysterious rhythms we are borne ineluctably in a never-ceasing drift of stars

[1] Conrad Fiedler *On Judging Works of Visual Art* translated by Henry Schaefer-Simmer and Fulmer Mood, University of California Press 1957 pp 48-49

and his whole argument depends on the same conception of art as

> a desire to wrest forms from the real world to which man is subject and to make them enter into a world of which he is the ruler.

The history of art is an epic struggle to give significance to life, to impose a meaning on visual experience. A style is the achievement of such significance:

> Every style . . . creates its own universe by selecting and incorporating such elements of reality as enable the artist to focus the shape of things on some essential part of man.[1]

Malraux, like Focillon before him, insists on the traditional, the autonomous nature of this formative activity; an artist's style is not born in a vacuum, but is rather a modification of immediately preceding styles. I think that Malraux underestimates the artist's direct experience of the visual world, especially the buried effects of such experience on the virgin sensibility in childhood; but in the main he supports Fiedler's point of view and sees the artist as 'a transformer of the meaning of the world'—as one whose style is the transformation of a material substance.

I must now return to the art of words, to literature, and consider whether style can be conceived, as Fiedler and Malraux conceived it in the visual arts, as a continuous working of the mind to bring order out of the chaos of appearances, to give signification to that world of experience which can never be

[1] *The Voices of Silence* translated by Stuart Gilbert, London and New York 1953 pp 213 to 334

totally expressed.[1] Is creative activity in literature also 'an entirely original and absolutely independent mental activity', having nothing in common with rational modes of cognition? If so, the purpose and style of criticism becomes something clearly different from the academic industry that now usurps its function.

What criticism has become in our time is clearly shown in the preface to the most considerable account of the subject now available. I refer to Professor Wellek's *History of Modern Criticism*. There it is stated that the term 'criticism' will be interpreted broadly to mean

> not only judgements of individual books and authors, 'judicial' criticism, practical criticism, evidences of literary taste, but *mainly* (and I emphasize the word) what has been thought about the principles and theory of literature, its nature, its creation, its function, its effects, its relations to the other activities of man, its kinds, devices and techniques, its origins and history.[2]

—a comprehensive definition into which, however, the word 'style' does not enter—presumably it has been fragmented into 'kinds, devices and techniques'. A phrase like 'the principles and theory of literature' expresses exactly the difference in the style of criticism that has been established for English literature in the past fifty years—I will presently explain

---

[1] cf. 'Poetry is a feat of style by which a complex of meaning is handled all at once.' William Wimsatt and Monroe Beardsley, The Intentional Fallacy, Ch. i of *The Verbal Icon*, University of Kentucky Press 1954, Noonday Press edition 1958 p 4

[2] René Wellek *A History of Modern Criticism* Jonathan Cape, London, and Yale University Press, New Haven 1955, i, p v

why I am so precise in my chronology. Such a phrase would not have been used by Hazlitt or Arnold, by Swinburne or Pater; and though it might have figured in some niche of Coleridge's *Opus Maximum*, we may be sure that principles and theory would have been subordinated to the 'one concentrating principle' of style. The science of Criticism, Coleridge wrote in one of his unpublished manuscripts,

> dates its restoration from the time when it was seen that an examination and appreciation of the end was necessarily antecedent to the formation of the rules, supplying at once the principle of the rules themselves, and of their application to the given subject.[1]

In other words, a scientific criticism is subordinate to an intuitive criticism. Or, to put the same thought in still other words derived from Coleridge, the proofs of original genius, which are the values that criticism should strive to reveal, intellectual life itself—these are only to be discerned by an exercise of sympathy that meets and mingles with the poet's own predominant passion.

I suggested just now that the New Criticism— which is, broadly speaking, a criticism pretending to scientific method—was about fifty years old. I had in mind as a determining date the foundation of the English Tripos at the University of Cambridge in 1917, but it may be that the history of the subject should be carried much further back, to the introduction of Medieval and Modern Languages into the curricula of British and American universities. It is

[1] Alice D. Snyder *Coleridge on Logic and Learning. With Selections from the Unpublished Manuscripts* New Haven 1930 p 110

doubtful if our researches into the origins of scientific criticism could halt this side of Herder, who, if not the first systematic critic of modern literature, was, as René Wellek says, 'certainly the one who has most clearly been the fountainhead of universal literary history'.[1] But Herder, to whom I believe we owe the definition of poetry as 'the music of the soul', would hardly have approved of his historical progeny. He was the great initiator, but alas, says Professor Wellek, his 'terminology is very loose; his concepts are shifting, his language is emotional and rhapsodical'. He left to others 'the task of formulating a new, coherent, systematic theory of poetry and literature'.

This new, coherent, systematic theory of poetry and literature was surely not formulated by Schiller or the Schlegels, certainly not by Goethe or Coleridge, nor by Arnold or Bagehot. It is a creation of our own uncreative age, and there is more than a suspicion that it is in some sense a cautious substitute for the activity of the imagination. Some years ago a disillusioned product of the system wrote a book called *The Muse in Chains*,[2] which was a description of the growth of English studies in the English-speaking countries. The Master of Jesus College has more recently written a book called *The Muse Unchained*,[3] which he describes as 'an

[1] For a masterly account of the significance of Herder in philosophy and criticism, see 'J. G. Herder' by Isaiah Berlin *Encounter* Vol xxv 1965 Nos. 1 July and 2 August

[2] Stephen Potter *The Muse in Chains* Jonathan Cape, London 1937

[3] E. M. W. Tillyard *The Muse Unchained* Bowes, London 1958

intimate account of the revolution in English studies at Cambridge'. What, we might legitimately ask, is the purpose, academic or otherwise, of formulating a systematic theory of poetry and literature, and making it the basis of instruction? Dr. Tillyard unchains his muse from what? In fact, from Languages; in effect, from that kind of scholarship that can only be exercised on a dead and dessicated body. Literature, it was felt (I am referring to the particular example of Cambridge, but the same development was taking place throughout the English-speaking world), literature was alive, and should be kept alive; its life should permeate the cloisters and classrooms. How could it be done?

At this point I must make a distinction, which I ought perhaps to have made at the beginning of this essay, between criticism and scholarship. In general it is a distinction between theory and fact, between opinion and hypothesis, between judgement and evidence. Criticism is comparative and evaluative; scholarship is accumulative and impartial. Criticism can bring order into confusion and clarity into obscurity, but it cannot impose on a vital and spontaneous process the rigid categories of a system. It remains, from its historical beginnings to its present manifestations, fluid, penetrating and yet constructive. It proceeds from motions of sympathy and pretences of identity: whereas scholarship is, or should be, external, impassive and even unmotivated. That much of it is pathologically obsessive may be recognized, but not necessarily regretted. There are more dangerous forms of lunacy.

Those idealists who wished to free the muse of

literature from the chains of language were not always clear about this distinction between criticism and scholarship. Dr. Tillyard confesses that English studies in Cambridge took shape in a very haphazard way. He himself had had a teacher of Classics who treated his subject 'in a literary way', which seems to have meant relating the classics of ancient literature to the greater body of world literature, plus a talk in the sixth form on literary criticism. Dr. Tillyard gives as a quite exceptional fact that he learned at school there was such a study as literary criticism. But he was quickly disillusioned when he went to Cambridge and found that the study of Classics would tolerate no such nonsense.

There is no need to relate the whole story: the English Tripos was established in 1917; a syllabus was agreed to—six papers on English Literature, Modern and Medieval; five papers on Early Literature (Anglo-Saxon, Norse, Celtic, Gothic) with some history—the early history and antiquities of Britain, for example. There were to be questions on language, metre, literary history and literary criticism, on life and thought. The School was successful beyond the dreams of its founders. Not merely was the School a success in the academic sense: it was an ideological success, the triumph of a philosophy—the anti-idealistic philosophy of G. E. Moore. As Dr. Tillyard says,

> It can hardly escape observation that Moore's turning away from the idealism of F. H. Bradley and his concentration on problems of meaning, on, for instance, the frequent ambiguity of apparently simple statements, were to have their analogue in the turning

away of criticism from a mystical emotionalism to the practice of linguistic analysis.

Practical criticism was born, the principles of it were announced to the world by Dr. I. A. Richards.

I am not going to maintain that the fecund vogue for analytical criticism, as Dr. Tillyard calls it, that then ensued has been altogether a bad thing, either for criticism or literature. When *The Principles of Literary Criticism* appeared in 1924, I welcomed it in a review in *The Criterion*[1] as 'an important contribution to the rehabilitation of English criticism— perhaps, because of its sustained scientific nature, the most important contribution yet made', and questioned only the lack of an adequate theory of imagination and of a moral perspective. I did not, to the best of my memory, review *Practical Criticism* when it appeared five years later, but by then I had begun to suspect that the English School at Cambridge had somehow taken a wrong turning; and the proliferation of its worst excesses in the United States was alarming.

The reason for past alarm and present despondency is given in a casual confession made by Dr. Tillyard in his history of the Cambridge School.

In one matter I differed from my two allies (Richards and M. D. Forbes). I minded more than they did about the way the undergraduates wrote. Here Q (Professor Sir Arthur Quiller-Couch) was sounder. He believed that, however humble the kind of writing, the way you wrote was part of what you said, and that to lower your standard anywhere was to offend against civilization. And there he had all my

[1] Vol. III 1925 pp 444-449

support . . . But though Q was sound in doctrine he did not do much about it. He lectured in his early days on the art of writing, but, having lectured, he could not be troubled to begin a campaign for getting his doctrines put into action. This among others is the reason why the chief sin of the Cambridge English School is that it has never insisted on a high enough standard in the writing of English.[1]

There you have the story of the Academic Fall, the expulsion of the critic from the Poetic Paradise. The sin denounced by Dr. Tillyard is the sin against the creative spirit and is not merely an offence against civilization, but the source of all the barbarism we now endure. A magnificent opportunity existed in Cambridge in 1917, but it was missed. This was the moment when the stylistic standard in English studies was lowered, never to be raised again. One may speculate in vain as to what would have happened, not only in Cambridge but in English schools throughout the world, if Q had been a little more energetic and Dr. Tillyard a good deal more intransigent.

It will be said, in justification of what did happen and of what now happens, that style is a subjective quality, unteachable, too intangible to be accurately assessed by examiners, too personal to conform to the ethic of objectivity. But it is against that ethic, of course, that my protest is made. Objectivity is the delusion of the scientists, the rationalist dogma that has led to a philosophy without content and a civilization without moral sensibility. Instead of introducing this bankrupt ideal into the study of litera-

[1] *Op. cit.* pp 91-92

ture, where it has no place, our English Schools
might have had the courage to assert and establish
an ethic of subjectivity, for on such an ethic, poetry
and the arts and all the spiritual values that constitute a civilization, ultimately depend.

What do we mean by an ethic of subjectivity? At
its simplest, Q's belief that the way we write is part
of what we say. Goethe said this more forcibly, more
elaborately, in a well-known aphorism: I have often
quoted it, but I will quote it again, for it is the *locus
classicus* of my whole philosophy of art:

> Whereas *simple imitation* flourishes under tranquil
> and satisfying conditions of existence, and whereas
> *mannerism* calls for a light touch and a fresh individu-
> ality, that which I call *style* rests on the deepest
> foundations of cognition, on the inner essence of
> things, in so far as this is given us to comprehend in
> visible and tangible forms.[1]

This is but a premonition of the theory of aesthetic
cognition that Fiedler was to take up and develop,
and which still awaits adequate recognition. There
are many alternative formulations of the idea—in
Coleridge, in Kierkegaard, in Keats's letters, in
Novalis and Arnold, in Swinburne and Pater, in
Henry James. According to this theory style cannot
be conceived as external to form, as decoration or
polish added to the expression of meaning. Style
is the shape and texture of thought itself, and no
utterance or inflexion of the written word but has

[1] '. . . so ruht der *Stil* auf den tiefsten Grundfesten der
Erkenntnis, auf dem Wesen der Dinge, insofern uns erlaubt ist,
es in sichtbaren und greiflichen Gestalten zu erkennen. *Sämt-
liche Werke* Stuttgart 1902-1907 vol. 33 p 56

its significance for communication and representation. Henry James, in writing about an author who has now fallen out of favour, Gabriele D'Annunzio, made this point in his own inimitable way, and I quote his remarks a little defiantly, to show that it is not a question of style being given importance by the weight of its message: style is its own virtue, not independent of meaning, but inevitably constituting whatever meaning is to be conveyed. But here is James on D'Annunzio's 'ample and exquisite style, his curious, various, inquisitive, always active employment of language':

> So close is the marriage between his power of 'rendering', in the light of the imagination, and whatever he sees and feels, that we should much mislead in speaking of his manner as a thing distinct from the matter submitted to it. The fusion is complete and admirable, so that, though his work is nothing if not 'literary', we see at no point of it where literature or where life begins or ends: we swallow our successive morsels with as little question as we swallow food that has by proper preparation been reduced to singleness of savour. It is brought home to us afresh that there is no complete creation without style any more than there is complete music without sound; also that when language becomes so closely applied and impressed a thing . . . the fact of artistic creation is registered at a stroke.[1]

You may protest that both Goethe and Henry James are speaking of artistic creation, and that criticism is a mundane activity exempt from the conditions that constitute the art of literature. But

[1] Henry James *Notes on Novelists* London 1914 pp 201-202

that is to make the vile distinction between an art that is expressive and a science that is cognitive. There is only one situation: man in the midst of his incomprehensible universe; and art and science are his surveying instruments. In so far as these instruments communicate through the medium of language, they have the same duty, which is to put the proper words in their proper places. But what a subtle exercise is implied by this simple phrase! The word 'proper' means originally private or peculiar to oneself, so we are thrown back on the personal equation and there is no objective science of style to help us. The style of the critic is the style of the man himself and renders with fidelity the substance and value of his thought.

This is not, of course, a plea for simplicity, desirable as that may be as an ideal. The existential situation of man is both obscure and complex, and that patient construction of a credible reality, which is the function of art, cannot be accomplished with a set of child's bricks. Not only is the nature of reality beyond our full comprehension, but those works of art that come nearest to its comprehension are inevitably in themselves somewhat intangible or elusive. Criticism may throw more light upon them, but their symbolic nature, their essence, defies our exact cognition. What is a mode of visual or poetic cognition cannot also be a mode of rational cognition.

It had been my intention to present some specimens of modern criticism as illustrations of its fall from grace, but the selection would be an act of reckless discrimination, and is it really necessary? We are all conscious of the stylistic gulf that separates our present academic exercises from such models of critical prose as Wordsworth's Preface to the *Lyrical Ballads*, Shelley's 'A Defence of Poetry', the twenty-second chapter of *Biographia Literaria*, Arnold's essay on Wordsworth, Bagehot's on Charles Dickens or Pater's on Coleridge. These are seminal occasions; and one has the certitude, as one reads such essays, that as Hazlitt said of Burke in another essay which I might have given as a touchstone, their words are the most like *things*: which is to say, that they constitute the reality they would describe.

It may be that in ascribing the decline in the style of criticism to the spirit of scientism that now prevails in our academies I am but exhibiting a prejudice of my own. I speak as a poet: I am not a member of the academic profession. The art of poetry is depressed and though the causes of its decline must be sought in social and economic developments which are beyond the control of critics, yet criticism must be held responsible for the present state of poetry in so far as it has betrayed its own highest ideal, which should be an artistic ideal. Professor Frye, in a passage which I quote at greater length on page 14, says truly in the 'Polemical Introduction' to his *Anatomy of Criticism*, that

> the presence of incommunicable experience in the centre of criticism will always keep criticism an art, as long as the critic recognizes that criticism comes out of it but cannot be built on it.

But it is not a question of bringing the direct experience of literature into the structure of criticism, which is to suppose, and wrongly suppose, that 'the swift intuitive certainty of good taste is infallible'. It is a question of proving in the substance of criticism that the critic is creative in his own mode of apprehension, and that he approaches more nearly to the communication of the incommunicable in the degree that his own instrument is subtle and refined, sensitive and above all sympathetic. For the secret of language, as Ruskin said, is the secret of sympathy, 'and its full charm is possible only to the gentle'.

Gentleness and charm—such are the disarming qualities we oppose to the bristling batteries of scientific criticism. I had intended this essay to be rigorous and unsparing; it would have been easy to have held up to ridicule some example of the graceless writing that passes for criticism in our schools. But it is a question of establishing the criterion rather than of applying it. Once style is accepted, not as an anachronism, nor as a vain rhetoric opposed to creative energy and intellectual integrity, but as the inevitable fusion of the quality of the mind and the mode of its expression, then judgement becomes inevitable and instinctive. Time and style, the scythe and the flail, work together in this field and the grain that endures is the living word.

4

THE DEFINITION OF COMEDY

IT was Hazlitt, in his *Lectures on the English Comic Writers*, who first used the word 'artificial' in speaking of Congreve. Charles Lamb immediately afterwards gave the word, in the same connection, a currency of charm and fashion. From that day to this the word 'artificial' has sufficed to explain Congreve and the school of comedy which he brought to perfection. It should be noted straightaway that the word is used in a commendatory, or at least an apologetic sense. Hazlitt thought the character of Millamant 'better adapted for the stage' (than that of Imogen or Rosalind) because 'it is more artificial, more theatrical, more meretricious'. Lamb, developing this suggestion, excused what he really thought an indulgence 'beyond the diocese of the strict conscience' by ascribing to the comedies of Wycherley and Congreve (in an essay by very name on the *Artificial* Comedy) an imaginary 'land of cuckoldry —the Utopia of gallantry, where pleasure is duty, and the manners perfect freedom'. Comedy thus became for him an inverse sort of idealism, in which actions and sentiments had their being on a plane quite removed from actuality and therefore quite remote in influence.

Hazlitt and Lamb were in a real dilemma. They

had boundless admiration for the wit and artistry of these comedies, but they could not reconcile them with the moral consciousness of their own age. Or, if this seems to put too much stress on *moral* consciousness, very much the same difficulty was involved by the romantic consciousness then equally rife. The moral code would balk at the profligacy of Wycherley's and Congreve's characters: the romantic code, in mute conspiracy, would shy at the cynical realism with which these authors treated the passion of love, or the feminine mind. Therefore a process known to the psychologist as 'rationalization' supervened and the theory of artificial comedy was elaborated. It was a plausible idea and the dilemma was effectively shelved in the subconscious mind.

By 1841 the moral consciousness had stiffened. The Victorian age was in full vigour and Macaulay, writing in that year, was able to dismiss Lamb's theory of artificial comedy as 'altogether sophistical' —not because he thought such a theory derogatory to the literary merits of the plays in question, but because he felt it to be a lame defence of a literature inherently perverse and corrupted.

'In the name of art, as well as in the name of virtue, we protest against the principle that the world of pure comedy is one into which no moral enters. If comedy be an imitation, under whatever conventions, of real life, how is it possible that it can have no reference to the great rule which directs life, and to feelings which are called forth by every incident of life? . . . But it is not the fact that the world of these dramatists is a world into which no moral enters. Morality constantly enters into that world, a sound morality, and an unsound morality; the sound morality to be insulted, derided, associated with everything mean and hateful; the unsound morality to be set off to every advantage, and inculcated by all methods, direct and indirect.'

And so on. With Macaulay's main contention we agree. The world of our comic dramatists *is* real and is meant to be real. Lamb's argument *is* altogether sophistical. But Macaulay's is something worse. It is heterodox criticism of the most subversive type. It is the utter confusion of morality and art. 'The question', says Macaulay, 'is simply this, whether a man of genius who constantly and systematically endeavours to make this sort of character attractive, by uniting it with beauty, and grace, dignity, spirit, a high social position, popularity, literature, wit, taste, knowledge of the world, brilliant success in every undertaking, does or does not make an ill use of his powers. We own that we are unable to understand how this question can be answered in any way but one.' But this, as applied to Congreve, and even to Wycherley, is a mis-statement of the position and a misunderstanding of the men. Before we can answer Macaulay's question, in a way he would be unable to understand, we must be clear as to what we intend by the function of comedy.

The distinction between wit and humour, which is the first essential of the matter, has often been attempted, but, except in a few sharp phrases of Meredith's, with no very satisfactory results. Hazlitt's antitheses are merely descriptive and in the manner of such criticism, end insignificantly.

'Humour is the describing the ludicrous as it is

in itself; wit is the exposing it, by comparing it or contrasting it with something else. Humour is, as it were, the growth of nature and accident; wit is the product of art and fancy. Humour, as it is shewn in books, is an imitation of the natural or acquired absurdities of mankind, or of the ludicrous in accident, situation and character; wit is the illustrating and heightening the sense of that absurdity by some sudden and unexpected likeness or opposition of one thing to another, which sets off the quality we laugh at or despise in a still more contemptible or striking point of view. . . . Wit hovers round the borders of the light and trifling, whether in matters of pleasure or pain. . . . Wit is, in fact, the eloquence of indifference. . . .'

Hazlitt also makes use of Congreve's own conception of humour as 'a singular and unavoidable manner of doing or saying anything, Peculiar and Natural to one Man only; by which his Speech and Actions are distinguished from those of other Men' (Letter to Mr. Dennis concerning Humour in Comedy). But this is using 'humour' in the rather special sense given to it by Ben Jonson and does not really touch the distinction between humour and wit. Such a 'humour' is rather the object on which humour in the general sense may be exercised. We must adopt some more precise distinction.

I would suggest one that may be readily used: humour differs from wit in the degree of action implied; or, to express the same idea psychologically, in the degree of introversion or extraversion expressed. The more the comic spirit resorts to activity or accident to gain its point, the more it tends to humour; and, in the contrary direction, the more the comic spirit seeks to achieve its effect in abstract or intellectual play, the better it merits the term wit. This distinction implies a no-man's-land where the categories overlap; and as a matter of fact it is in such a no-man's-land that some of the best English comedies, such as Wycherley's *Country Wife* and *Plain Dealer*, have their peculiar existence.

This pragmatical distinction conforms to the guiding idea of Meredith's *Essay on Comedy*—the idea of comedy as the humour of the mind.

'The comic poet is in the narrow field, or enclosed square of the society he depicts; and he addresses the still narrower enclosure of men's intellects, with reference to the operation of the social world upon their characters. [And again:] The Comic, which is the perceptive, is the governing spirit, awakening and giving aim to the powers of laughter, but it is not to be confounded with them: it enfolds a thinner form of them, differing from satire, in not sharply driving into the quivering sensibilities, and from humour, in not comforting them and tucking them up. . . .'

But it is time to return to Macaulay—and then to Congreve. Macaulay's moral outburst will now be seen to involve a misconception of comedy and indeed of all art. It is also based on a mis-statement of fact: The 'morality' of Congreve's plays is far from being that of 'low town-rakes' and 'dashing Cyprians'. One could search in vain, even in the sort of literature approved by Macaulay, for characters more agreeable than Valentine and Angelica, or indeed, for a play more generally salutary in its theme than *Love for Love*. In *The Double Dealer* the true lovers, Mellefont and Cynthia are perfect exemplars of virtue, vigorously contrasted against the villainy of Maskwell and Lady Touchwood. The conventional propriety of the Mourning Bride has never been questioned, except by Jeremy Collier, who descends to the lowest level of his crassness in the attempt. Voltaire's astonishment at the 'cleanness' of Congreve is well known. But this kind of justification, though possible, is otiose. Art is a general activity, and any limitations to its scope are meaningless and arbitrary. It includes in its field of vision the immoral as well as the moral—and all other qualities of the human mind. The question of values is relative and only concerns the artist in a formative sense; and such values are the general values of culture, among which the moral values have no special precedence. They are part of that perceptive sense which is the fund of character; and it is the quality of the artist's mind, as Henry James said,[1] that determines the deepest quality of his art. But to require, in the manner of Macaulay, that the artist's moral conscience should sit in judgement as his characters take shape in his imagination, is a stupidity of the most elementary kind, showing a complete misunderstanding of the function of art and of the psychology of the artist. It was the same stupidity that caused Macaulay to heap ridiculous praise on Collier's *Short View of the Immorality and Profaneness of the English Stage*, '. . . whose hysterical

---

[1] 'There is one point at which the moral sense and the artistic sense lie very near together; that is in the light of the very obvious truth that the deepest quality of a work of art will always be the quality of the mind of the producer.'

screaming and scoldings were to some degree per-
petuated by being condensed in the vapid and lack-
lustre philippics of one who was both pedant and
prig, Thomas Babington Macaulay'.[1]

There is every evidence that Congreve was no
mere genius of the instinctive order, but a critical
writer fully conscious of the nature of his powers. I
have already quoted from the Letter to Dennis; there
are more passages of the same nature to be culled.
In his reply to Collier's attack, Congreve fell back on
the Aristotelian definition of comedy as 'an Imitation of the worst sort of People . . . in respect to
their Manners'. Again, in the Dedication of the
Double Dealer he had replied to the accusation that
he represented some Women as vicious and affected
in these words:

'How can I help it? It is the business of a Comick
poet to paint the Vices and Follies of Humane kind;
and there are but two sexes that I know, viz. *Men*
and *Women*, which have a Title to Humanity: And
if I leave one half of them out, the work will be imperfect. I should be very glad of an opportunity to
make my Complement to those Ladies who are
offended; but they can no more expect it in a Comedy
than to be Tickled by a Surgeon when he's letting 'em
blood. They who are Virtuous or Discreet should not
be offended, for such Characters as these distinguish
them, and make their Beauties more shining and
observ'd: And they who are of the other kind, may
nevertheless pass for such, by seeming not to be dis-
pleased or touched with the Satyr of this *Comedy*.'

[1] Montague Summers in his Introduction to *The Complete
Works of William Congreve* Nonesuch Press, London 1923 p 30

This is very like Meredith's spirit of Comedy. The weakness, if weakness there is, lies in the word *satire* —not that it is used by Congreve with any special deliberation. But it marks a certain lack of perception, least noticeable in Congreve among all his contemporaries, but still present. 'Our English school', writes Meredith, 'has not clearly imagined society; and of the mind hovering above congregated men and women, it has imagined nothing.' Further on in the same essay, Meredith quotes Landor: 'Genuine humour and true wit require a sound and capacious mind, which is always a grave one', and he then remarks: 'Congreve had a certain soundness of mind; of capacity, in the sense intended by Landor, he had little.' This charge is well placed and skilfully supported by chapter and verse; and must for the present be recorded as the final word on Congreve. Of Congreve's character we derive from his letters and from contemporary accounts a fairly real conception; it lives best in Swift's epithet 'unreproachful'. But it adds nothing to the critical question. Of his mind we know less. From such writings as the *Amendments to Mr. Collier's False and Imperfect Citations* and the *Discourse on the Pindarique Ode* we can judge it to have been learned and even a little pedantic. His lack of capacity would seem to have been rather in the nature of a defect of vision. But vision is an idle word which we must try to make a little more precise.

The comic spirit, in Meredith's sense, is subject to three declensions or diminutions of effect. It can become, as Satire, angry and acidulated—an instrument of invective and not of persuasion. It can become, as Irony, indirect and uncertain. And as

Humour it can identify itself with its object, revelling in the situation rather than offering any solution of it. Congreve is alert enough not to stray into any of these by-ways of the comic spirit; but it cannot be said that his conceptions are always 'purely comic, addressed to the intellect'. The epithet that fits them best is *cynical*: it is not the calm curious eye of Meredith's spirit, but the calm *in*curious eye appropriate to another attitude.

Of cynicism one can say little but that it is the spirit of comedy without gravity, without profundity. When we pass from Congreve to Molière, or even to Meredith himself, we have left an arid for a rich amusement. Perhaps there are epochs in history, as certainly there are periods in life, when no attitude but cynicism is possible, because despair is too inevitable. And perhaps the end of the Seventeenth Century was such an epoch, as our own day seems to be another. In any case, such a supposition would go far to explain the only defect of Congreve's comedy, and whilst explaining, make it forgiveable.

But in the process of explanation we must never forget the real achievement. Congreve's quality at its best, in *The Way of the World*, is of a texture, undeniably intellectual, that baffles the would-be analyst. To begin with, it is impossible to trace it down to a passage or a phrase. It lives in the characters, who are created by suggestion rather than by description. It becomes more a matter of localized fact in the extremely efficient and finely rhythmed style. This one might illustrate at random from any of the four comedies. A soliloquy of Mirabell's from *The Way of the World* will serve (Millamant has just left him with a 'when you have done thinking of that, think of me'):

'*Mira.* I have something more—Gone—Think of you! To think of a Whirlwind, tho' 'twere in a Whirlwind, were a Case of more steady Contemplation; a very tranquility of Mind and Mansion. A Fellow that lives in a Whirlwind, has not a more whimsical Dwelling than the Heart of a Man that is lodg'd in a Woman. There is no Point of the Compass to which they cannot turn, and by which they are not turn'd; and by one as well as by another; for Motion not Method is their Occupation. To know this, and yet continue to be in Love, is to be made wise from the Dictates of Reason, and yet persevere to play the Fool by the force of Instinct.—O here comes my pair of Turtles—What, billing so sweetly! Is not Valentine's Day over with you yet?'

I have selected this passage for the perfect management of transitions, for the mastery of phrase, and for the apt use of rhythm and alliteration; but I doubt if I could find a better one to illustrate the real basis of thought, or, as we should perhaps say nowadays, of psychological observation, that after all sets Congreve's comedies apart from those of his contemporaries, not excepting even Wycherley. The oppositions of Motion and Method, of Reason and Instinct, though embodied in comic play, are not there by chance; and for their date they strike a strangely modern note, a note that sounds again and again as we read through these plays, making Congreve significant to our own generation in a sense only shared by Donne among the English writers of the seventeenth century.

5

THE DISCIPLES OF DIDEROT

Bless me, sir, a terrible progeny! they belong to the tribe of *Incubi*.

The Rev. Dr. Folliott, in *Crotchet Castle*

WE may safely leave aside any general enquiry into the dramatic theories of Diderot: they make on the whole rather a wearisome display of dialectic, only redeemed by Diderot's loquacious instinct: the father of the encyclopaedias, even in his most encyclopaedic moments, managed to vivify his prose with the accent of his tongue—which, if we are to believe his contemporaries, was by far the best witness to his real powers. But on one question of dramatic art Diderot remains a very authentic voice; and the voice is the voice of a prophet. The lesser theologians who derive from his original gospel still thrive with that luxuriance so characteristic of later theologies of every kind. For this reason it seems worth while to isolate the particular theory to which I refer: to see the shape it took in the mind of Diderot; to follow its reverberations in the larger critical intelligence of Lessing; to connect it with the conditions that gave it birth; and finally to ask whether the theory has any general validity to-day and why it should continue to be imposed as a dogma and an inhibition to genius.

Diderot had a romantic dislike for anything approaching a systematic exposition of his ideas. 'O faiseurs de règles générales, que vous ne connoissez guère l'art, et vous avez peu de ce génie qui a produit les modèles sur lequel vous avez établi ces règles, qu'il est le maître d'enfreindre quand il lui plaît!' So he exclaims midway in his own rambling essay *De la Poésie Dramatique*, and we know the insufferable systems he had in mind. But Diderot carried his formlessness to the verge of obscurity: we get lost in the maze of his irrelevancies and divagations and turn with relief to some such summary abstract as that made by Emile Faguet in his *Dix-huitième Siècle*. We cannot, however, in that way dispense with Diderot. The essential Diderot is precisely in those divagations which, having little to do with the matter in hand, carry, however, a sudden illumination into the mind. As when he writes: 'Les plans se forment d'après l'imagination; les discours, d'après la nature.' Or as when he draws this distinction between satire and comedy: 'La satire est d'un tartuffe, et la comédie est du Tartuffe. La satire poursuit un vice. S'il n'y avait eu qu'une ou deux Précieuses Ridicules, on en aurait pu faire une satire, mais non pas une comédie.' The whole of the *Paradoxe sur le Comédien* is packed with observations on the art of acting—some of them derived directly from Garrick —which modern actors might still study with advantage. And this essay is the more interesting because its particular theme, namely, that the actor plays best, even in scenes of great passion or emotion, when still retaining his self-possession, is in direct contradiction to the general tenor of Diderot's naturalism.

Three main ideas emerge from the voluble chaos. One we may dismiss as no longer alive—the contention that the dramatist should interest himself in the *conditions* rather than the *characters* of his creations; that is, in the attributes of fatherhood, rather than in the personality of a father. It was one of those futile attempts, always doomed to failure because they are directed from some standpoint of external theory, to limit the subject-matter of art. Diderot's second idea—that the theatre should act as a moral agent—we may dismiss for other reasons. Diderot held this idea very strongly as, indeed, did most of his contemporaries, including Voltaire. It was imagined, I think, that the direct contact between the living agents of the drama (the actors) and the audience was of an immediacy unknown in any other forms of art, and man being so much impelled by imitative instincts, here, in the theatre, was the ideal field for the inculcation of the virtues. I doubt if one could find a modern critic (so sensitive have they become) to defend a theory so bald in its utilitarian motives; but if we have by now shelved this problem, it is not so much that we have got rid of it by solving it, or that we have dismissed it as insoluble. It is rather that we have given it a different incidence. We have subjectivized it. We no longer expect (or even condone) the direct moral purpose in art, but, if we have any critical principles of adequate reach, we demand a quality in the mind of the artist which works out, in the end, as the moral equivalent of this purpose. That is to say, the work of art no longer expresses a moral purpose: it implies one. This is perhaps a subtle distinction, but it is of the essence of the modern critical position.

Diderot's third plea, and his most insistent one, was for a more natural mode in the theatre. As Emile Faguet has remarked, what is natural in one age is conventional in the next—'and this is necessary, since, only to maintain the same degree of convention, one must react against the conventional every fifty years'. For Diderot, naturalism implied many things—all of them at that time of a revolutionary nature. He would abolish the stilted alexandrine of the traditional drama and substitute the natural prose of speech; he would do away with the tedious formality of the *discourse* in drama and introduce instead the quick action and animated gestures of normal life; and then, in a large manner, he pleaded for the *genre sérieux* in comedy and for the domestic theme in general.

It is not part of my intention to trace the origin of these ideas (they mostly came from England) or to examine the causes, mainly social, which determined them. It is more to my purpose to observe that the general procedure so cynically foreshadowed by Emile Faguet does not in this case seem to have been followed. It is now about one hundred and seventy years since these theories were enunciated and we still have critics who write as though these things had been in the essence of drama for ever, and as though Elizabethan tragedy, and much else before and after not conforming to the naturalistic standard, had been but a regrettable aberration from some inevitable norm. But before discussing the modern situation I would like to glance at the immediate reception accorded to Diderot's naturalistic theories by the clear intelligence of Lessing.

The *Hamburg Dramaturgy* is the modern *Poetics* —at least, since Aristotle there is no work devoted to the theory of the drama so illuminating and suggestive as this series of occasional criticisms given to the world between 1767 and 1769. The whole burden of the work is: Back to Aristotle!—and Lessing does not hesitate to acknowledge that he considers the *Poetics* as infallible as the *Elements* of Euclid (in a Euclidean world!). The French, on the other hand, he conceived as having misapprehended the rules of ancient drama: from Corneille and Racine to Voltaire they had built up a structure on misinterpretations and mistranslations of the text of Aristotle, and on a perverse emphasis of his incidental illustrations, regardless of the general logic of the argument. The state of the drama which Diderot, with his empirical sense, conceived as unnatural, Lessing conceived as false learning, false logic, false history. From this point of view Diderot, too, must be brought up against the infallible principles of Aristotle and reproved for the excess of his reactions. The fresh sight that animated Diderot's mind came from England—from English philosophy with its realistic bent and from English plays with their life despite the rules: and this same inrush of reality was operative in Lessing's mind and in Germany very generally at that time. But Lessing kept his head. We must not, he said, confound all rules with bad rules, or count all discipline as pedantry. There was a real danger, he felt, of wantonly throwing away the experience of all past times and demanding from the poet that he should discover his art anew.

Diderot, in the course of his distinction between character and conditions, had been drawn into a facile generalization to the effect that whilst the characters of a tragedy must be in some degree particular, those of a comedy are always general.

'The comic genus has species, the tragic has individuals. The hero of a tragedy is such and such a man; he is Regulus or Brutus or Cato, and no other. The prominent persons in a comedy, on the other hand, must represent a large number of mankind.' This assertion of Diderot's aroused all Lessing's vigour and he had little difficulty in showing that not only is there no justification for such a dogma in the *Poetics*, but also that such a doctrine would be contrary to the very principles of art. It is *art*, of course, in a very classical sense, but precisely there is the difference between these two minds. Diderot's plea is a plea for the personal equation in art: it is the plea of an incipient romantic.

Lessing, however, frankly admits that Aristotle does not altogether solve the problem. There are two senses of generality: in the first sense a general character means a character in which what has been observed in one or more individuals is welded together; and Lessing calls this type a *composite* (*überladen*) character. 'It is more the personified idea of a character than a characterised person.'[1] In the other sense

[1] The quotations from *Hamburgische Dramaturgie* are given in Helen Zimmern's translation (London 1879), but I have taken the liberty of making one or two very slight amendments.

a general character means a character in which an average or mean proportion has been abstracted from many or all individuals—that is, a *typical (gewöhnlicher)* character. Aristotle's καθόλου is obviously generality in this second sense. It seems to have been left to Ben Jonson to elaborate the first conception—the embodiment of abstract character. a real distinction? Can the same character illustrate

The possibility of two such conceptions leaves Lessing in a state of doubt and indecision. Is there both the composite and the typical abstraction, and what is the value of the *individual* after all? Lessing left the problem unsolved; and it may appear remote enough at this day—a distinction not worth reviving, belonging to the dead logomachy of dramatic theory. But there are two things to bear in mind: first, that if we are to emerge from our present confusion in drama, we must return to distinctions of which perhaps this is one. Secondly, if we can now *solve* the problem, it will make a difference to its importance. It may be that in modern psychology, especially as it relates to the classification of types, we shall find a solution of the problem that baffled Lessing. 'What then?' the modern dramatist will be tempted to ask. 'Assuming that your psychological criticism does establish a single generality—what then? I create personalities and little do I care for your *types*, so long as my creations *live*.' It would only show how difficult it is to get the modern dramatist (or the modern dramatic critic) even to consent to the terms of classical art. It would be quite hopeless to expect him to draw a distinction between his function, as he so largely formulates it, and the function of, say, the novelist. But if once the liaison I foresee is established between criticism and psychology, then the individualist in dramatic art will find how probing the instruments of criticism can be.

Lessing's cautious response to the naturalism of Diderot is shown in other ways. But in some measure he can accept the new ideas readily, because though for Diderot they may express an immediate revolt against the absurdities of Voltaire, for Lessing they are more than this: they are a return to the 'infallible principles'. Thus 'Diderot is not wrong in pronouncing his thoughts on the superfluity and poverty of all uncertain expectations and sudden surprises to be as new as they are valid. They are new in regard to their abstraction, but very old in regard to the patterns from which they are abstracted. . . .' But it is sad to observe that where Lessing and Diderot agree, the modern naturalist elects to differ. There is an almost total unawareness of this consideration in modern plays and in modern dramatic criticism. Suspense, sustained excitement, surprise, and innocent deception are the foundations of the modern playwright's craft. And this craft is, of course, but one more reflection of the extensive vulgarity of the modern mind. Lessing refers us to Euripides. Euripides was so certain of himself that he almost showed his spectators the goal whither he would lead them. The gratification of a childish curiosity was the least of the pretensions of his art. His aim was to awaken emotions in the spectator 'not so much by that which should occur, as by the mode in which it should occur'. Can the modern dramatists appreciate that distinction? Can they understand that art does not begin until interest is at an end? But why make this rhetorical pretence? There is no question. The dramatist is no longer a poet: the *mode* of art is not even a consideration for him. His aim is to satisfy an interest, to 'pander' to a curiosity; above all to supply a commercial article to be played in a commercial theatre before a commercial audience. The circle is complete. Every interest is satisfied and the dissentient voice is half-ashamed of its lonely reverberations.

A minor agreement between Lessing and Diderot is found in the question of natural diction. Lessing could not deny that 'every passion has its own eloquence'. Aristotle would not deny it. And Lessing nowhere shows his sensible qualities so openly as in this simple acceptance of Diderot's attitude. The least inclination to pedantry or conservativism would have caused him to halt here; but the criterion, in this and equally in his acceptance of Aristotle, was logic and commonsense. 'There can never be feeling with a stilted, chosen, pompous language. It is not born of feeling, it cannot evoke it. But feeling agrees with the simplest, commonest, plainest words and expression. . . .' And here for once Lessing and Diderot have little to teach the modern dramatist, who has not added pomposity or affectation of language to his other faults. But it is a negative virtue: he is not pompous nor is he ever sublime.

The main energy of Lessing, however, was reserved for a re-statement of Aristotle's theory of *catharsis*. Here again one may feel an absence of relevance in this 'Serbonian bog' of criticism. Does Aristotle's theory mean anything to-day in modern terms? Has it any bearing at all on the function of modern drama?

Lessing realized that the only justification for drama as a distinct form of art lay in its direct appeal to social emotions. The poem and the prose fiction, on the other hand, operate individually. Aristotle's theory—that the function of drama is the correction and refinement of the emotions of pity and fear—is based on the psychological fact that these emotions are most thoroughly excited, are, in fact, only complete when aroused in a social unit: the unanimous group, the representative herd. That at any rate must be the modern justification for Aristotle's empirical selection of these two particular emotions. What Aristotle meant by the process of catharsis is precisely the point upon which so much wasted intellect has been expended. The view adopted by Lessing, and the only reasonable view at the time, was that by vicarious experience our pity and our fear, and all connected with them, become 'purified'. In Lessing's day there was no science of human behaviour adequate to account for either the process or the result. But modern psychology could, I think, give a fairly acceptable explanation—one that would not only restore the theory of Aristotle to its former standing, but would add fresh significance to this extraordinarily prescient hypothesis and reinstate it as a final criterion. It would reason that the instincts of pity and fear are primal instincts of man in his social aggregation; that these instincts in a healthy community must have expression; that direct expression is denied by the elaborate manners of civilization; and that vicarious expression can and must be given imaginary play. The drama thus becomes a sublimation of social instincts: a safety valve against undue pressures on the fabric of civilization.

We see how tolerantly, in these various gages, Lessing holds the balance between the extreme naturalism of Diderot (with its wider reverberations in the theories of Rousseau) and the fine logic of Aristotle's system. Lessing's great achievement, in fact, was to direct the growing turbulence of romanticism towards the static truths of classical dogma. 'In nature', he wrote in one of his most significant passages, 'everything is connected, everything is interwoven, everything changes with everything, everything merges from one into another. But such endless variety (*unendliche Mannichfaltigkeit*) is only a play for an infinite spirit. In order that finite spirits may have their share of this enjoyment, they must have the power to set up arbitrary limits; they must have the power to eliminate and to guide their attention at will. This power we exercise at all moments of our life; without this power there would be no life for us; from too many various feelings we should feel nothing, we should be the constant prey of present impressions, we should dream without knowing what we dream. The purpose of art is to save us this abstraction in the realms of the beautiful and to render the fixing of our attention easy to us. All in nature that we might wish to abstract in our thoughts from an object or a combination of various objects,

F

be it in time or in place, art really abstracts for us, and accords us this object or this combination of various objects as purely and tersely as the sensations they are to provoke allow.'

Diderot had a mere glimmering of these truths, but it was a real light. 'Nature may indeed have her sublime moments; but I think if anyone can be sure of seizing their sublimity and fixing it, it is he who has plumbed them with imagination or with genius, and has then expressed them with *sang-froid*' (*Paradoxe sur le Comédien*).

Lessing's attitude prepared the way for Goethe, Lessing in many ways made Goethe possible. But the *sang-froid* of Diderot? It was engulfed not only in Diderot's own chaos, but in the unrestrained tide for which he, in his way, was the precursor. In the vortex that followed we see only one figure clutching at this frail straw of *sang-froid*: it is a frail straw, but it has carried Henri Beyle into modern consciousness and given his work a significance beyond the limits of his time.

These rather random comments may perhaps now be drawn into relation with present issues. If I take William Archer as an English representative disciple of Diderot, I do so quite alive to the dangers attending such a 'dated' choice. Archer's opinions, expressed so forcibly in the book which we may regard as the summary of his life's work,[1] are so sparkling with crotchets that there is a possibility of the critic's indignation spending itself on the unrelated opinions

[1] William Archer *The Old Drama and the New: an Essay in Re-valuation* Heinemann London and Cambridge, Mass., 1923

rather than on the essential errors that lie underneath. But I must select Archer not only because he was a most lively champion of modern drama ('modern' in a retrospective sense), but also because his work as a critic had a formative influence of considerable extent on that drama. He, more aptly than anyone else, denotes and personifies the period from 1890 to 1920 —a period of genuine activity and undoubtedly of healthy renewal, but a period also, surely, of dreadful limitations. But these limitations did not exist for Archer: he honestly thought the generation of Pinero, Barrie, Shaw and Galsworthy probably superior to any other generation of playwrights in the history of English literature. And his prejudice did not spring from lack of knowledge—but did perhaps spring from too much knowledge of a specialized kind.

Shakespeare was a great inconvenience to Archer: Shakespeare had always to be made an exception to his bold generalizations—to all save one, for Shakespeare, despite his greatness as a poet, is not to be considered so intelligent or thought-provoking as Shaw or Ibsen. He was a 'stupendous genius' but *not* a 'colossal intellect'—a distinction I fail to make, though Archer says they are 'totally different things'. Shakespeare was 'content to live in a stationary world'; he was not 'alive to the great idea which differentiates the present age from all that have gone before—the idea of progress'. Here Archer betrays himself. This 'great idea', unknown to Shakespeare —was it not equally unknown to Aeschylus and Euripides, to Racine and Molière? Was it, in fact, known to anyone before Diderot and Rousseau invented it and an evolutionary philosophy perfected it? This is not the place to discuss the merits of the idea of progress: I would merely suggest that as an idea it has no more special precedence, apart from the cupidity of human desires, than any other idea— the idea of fatality, for example, or the idea of eternal recurrence. To think otherwise only betrays the humanistic prejudices on which this attitude of William Archer's is based, and from which his other more particular prejudices take their shape.

Our representative modernist lays down three tests of dramatic worth. One, that drama should say and mean something, does not need discussion: to anyone but a 'pure aesthete' it is a test too obvious to be in question. The second test requires an affirmative answer to the following question:

'Is the story developed, and are the characters presented, in such a way as to make the best use of the mechanism of the theatre, and to beget in the audience, in high intensity, those emotions of growing interest, suspense, anticipation, sudden and vivid realization, which it is the peculiar privilege of drama to produce?'

I have already dealt with the notion of suspense. Aesthetically it seems to me to involve a vulgar intention and for that reason I believe it was obviated by the classical dramatists. The other matter involved in this test—the full use of the mechanism of the theatre—I also believe to be beset with error. I think it should be an incontrovertible principle that the drama dictates to the theatre and not the theatre to the drama. That a poet should ignore the *essentials* of the stage is, of course, folly; but these esentials are extremely simple and extremely obvious. The rest is technical obscurantism. The attitude is usually bolstered up by the classical instances of Shakespeare and Molière—both actors and stage-managers and *therefore* good playwrights. But an occasional coincidence does not prove a rule or sanction a generalization. A host of utterly banal playwright-actors and playwright-managers weigh down the scale against Shakespeare and Molière. The real danger underlying this demand is that the imagination should be intimidated by the technicalities of stage machinery and by the supposed necessity of any mechanical or conventional properties. But this question is closely related to that involved in Archer's first and most insistent test.

'The theatre of all ages', he writes, 'is a machine devised, or rather developed, for the purpose of presenting to an assemblage of human beings imitations of human life, and thereby awakening a certain order of emotions which cannot be aroused in an equal degree by any other means'. That this won't do as a definition of Greek tragedy is obvious even to William Archer: he therefore makes the baffling distinction that 'Greek tragedy was not a realistic, but a consistent, imitation'. This is again a distinction without a difference—or rather, the words fail to express any distinction at all; they merely avoid the issue. In what possible sense can an imitation be realistic and not consistent? The point need not be pressed, for though he neglects the difficulty presented by Greek tragedy, Archer has no hesitation in applying his test to our own Elizabethan drama. The result is bloody in the extreme: not a reputation—'Shakespeare apart'—survives the ordeal.

That two centuries have been totally astray; that intelligences as acute as Lamb's, Coleridge's, and Swinburne's were utterly at sea; that the modern apologists for the Elizabethans are mere 'aesthetic paradox-mongers'—all these things are possible. But they are not likely, and Archer had not the gift of persuading people either by imaginative expression or logical argument. His fallacy seems to begin with a strange historical misconception of the use of the word 'imitation': he gave it the sense (and the epithet) of *pure* imitation, and by this implied the exactest photographic and phonographic representationalism—no other words will suffice for his extraordinarily bourgeois conception. Only a radical misunderstanding of the very nature of art could have supported him in the long analysis he made on the basis of his blind theory. He did not understand that all truly imaginative art 'functions' at a remove from reality. As in painting the artist selects from the disordered elements present in his direct vision, working his selected details into some pattern or abstraction, so in literature the poet creates his formal design, his stylized expression. Because his instinct is to 'create', his materials must be 'plastic'— his will is free. Archer, of course, saw that there was a difference, quality for quality, between the old drama and the new; this difference he ascribed to 'passion' and 'exaggeration' expressed in lyrical poetry; this poetry he thought he could dissociate entirely from the drama; and the dramatic essentials 'left over' were—pure imitation, technical efficiency, intellectual content. But it is not merely a question of occasional lyric utterance: modern drama, though it may answer to Archer's three essentials, and though it may eschew lyric utterance, lacks something else. It lacks the power to transmute its materials; it burns at a low temperature and with little light. It does not lift us into that other world which is the world of imaginative logic. That world is only seen when habitual ways are stopped, when the unwitting receptivity of sights and sounds is replaced by a heightened awareness of the unreal reality of existence. Then the mind of the inspired dancer does indeed become identified with his god.[1]

[1] 'It is very tempting,' writes William Archer in a note, 'to identify *imitation* with the Greek *mimesis* (applied in the main to the *ethos*, or character, of ordinary human beings). . . . But it appears on enquiry that the Greek words have no exact equivalent in English . . . *mimesis* meant originally "the state of mind of the inspired dancer representing or becoming his god. . . ." ' (*The Old Drama and the New* p 4)

6

THE DIALOGUE

IT was Landor's opinion that 'the best writers in
every age have written in dialogue'; but it is curious
how little, apart from the classifications of the
Platonists, has been written *about* the dialogue. No
attempt seems ever to have been made to define the
principles of such a literary form; and while it is a
method much used by a disciplined cast of mind, it
has scarcely become one of classical precision. Perhaps if we were wise we should rejoice in one field left
unmown by the blades of pedantry and logic; but
categories are dear to the critic, and a short essay in
eliminations may not be without interest to the
general reader.

A cursory review of 'the best writers' reveals a use
of three distinct kinds of dialogue, agreeing only in
the superficial appearance of the printed page. There
is (i) the dialogue of ideas, in which the speakers are
but embodiments of points of view; such a dialogue
is exemplified in the characteristic work of Plato,
Berkeley, Leopardi, Renan, and in our own time,
Paul Valéry. To this category we might add, in so far
as it ever becomes an artistic form, the dialogue of
instruction, such as Fénelon's *Dialogues on Eloquence*. Next there is (ii) the dialogue of wit, which,

though it has some idea in the background, tends not to expose this idea in the direct manner of Plato, but rather to get its effect indirectly by ironic ridicule or happy expression. This is the method of Lucian and of Fontenelle. Lastly there is (iii) the dialogue whose purpose is to exhibit character and personality; and this, of course, is the method largely practised by Landor.

It seems hopeless to reduce all this diversity to any common rationale or 'dialogic'. But one principle at least is essential to all the methods, and is present from the very beginning of the form. Plato is said to have been inspired by the lost Sicilian mimes of Sophron and Epicharmus, but it is likely that he merely found there the suggestion and not the substance of the form. For we must at once recognize that in Plato the dialogue has been purged of its dramatic nature. The *Phaedo*, as a narrative, is intensely dramatic ; as a dialogue it is a supreme example of de-dramatization. It is not merely that, as Jowett says, 'no dialogue has a greater unity of subject and feeling'; but this effect is itself secured by the formal construction of the dialogue as such. It is, most notably, a dialogue within a dialogue: Phaedo, who was present at the death of Socrates, relates the events and discussions that accompanied it to Echecrates of Phlius. The 'tragedy' is not merely given a distance in time and place, but is heard indirectly and through the channel of one unifying mind. We have, indeed, a sense of intense pathos, but it is abiding: it begins with the first words of Echecrates and ends only with that calm death and Phaedo's simple epitaph. The philosophical resignation of Socrates is like a key-note penetrating to the very essence of the aesthetic form in which it is embodied; till the dialogue itself is abstracted to a region of passionless integrity. Could any other form achieve this effect: give the same variety without expense of unity and the same intensity with such evenness, such grace, such absence of melodramatic violence? But the *Phaedo* is too exceptional to be a pattern: it seems, in its plentitude and exactitude, to live on the very limits or boundaries of its form. The norm has a more definite nucleus: an extreme of formal necessities separated by a wide enough gap from neighbouring categories. And at the nucleus is the idea. The *Phaedo*, too, has its idea: there is not merely the motive or theme, which is the immortality of the soul, but there is the underlying assumption, common to all profound philosophies, but never so perfectly exemplified as here, that the service of abstractions must dominate the practice of life. But in the *Phaedo* there is, as we have seen, something more than the idea—there is a narrative. Yet for perfection the dialogue need not have more than ideas. If the essential of drama is the portrayal of action, then the essential of dialogue is the creative activity of ideas—ideas in action, one might say. But not embodied action itself. In this fact is the first and most distinct principle of the art.

But merely to contrast action and ideas is perhaps not enough in the way of distinction. When we descend to the actual construction of a form of literary composition, such as drama, we find that its essence is not so much in its subject-matter as in the manner of the treatment of that subject-matter. We come precisely to those questions of diction, stress and rhythm so repugnant to the mere appreciator of literature, and so necessary to the real critic. It has been suggested in an ingenious dialogue,[1] which is in itself an illustration of our theme, that 'what makes a work dramatic is not so much its obvious shape, as the structure of its changes of motion. . . . The dramatic moment is that at which a change of speed intrudes.' This dynamic definition will suit our purpose very well. We shall lay it down as an axiom that the perfect dialogue has an evenness of motion within which the *dénouement* of idea makes its maximum effect; its outer 'speed' does not change, or only slightly, like the fountain that holds a ball in merry suspense.

Some happy chance or intuition has saved most of our authors from the dramatic fallacy. Diderot naturally, in his experimental fashion, comes nearest to disproving the principle. *Le Neveu de Rameau* illustrates as well as any other dialogue the play and counterplay of ideas, but it is interspersed with elaborate 'stage directions'—to a degree, in fact, quite foreign to drama. It rather approaches to narrative form and has been credited with effect on the history of fiction. It is picturesque and human, and in some ways the most interesting of all Diderot's writings; but considered as a dialogue (it is rather a monologue) the form, aiming at the development of ideas or the revelation of character, is in no way heightened or quickened, but quite overladen, by its explanatory devices. But it is in some sort an anticipation of Landor, and for this reason is perhaps more interesting than the less

[1] Bonamy Dobrée *Histriophone* Hogarth Press, London 1925

original dialogues which Diderot wrote in the elenctic manner of Plato. These, however, we must not despise, for Diderot had wit as well as logic, and everywhere, but especially in *Le Rêve de D'Alembert* (and its audacious *Suite*) we have evidence of Fontenelle's happy influence.

In the dramatic category we should also reckon Swift's *Polite Conversation*, a dialogue ridiculing the cant phrases of the time; but it is not strictly speaking a dialogue of ideas, and the fact that though published simply as a literary dialogue, it was nevertheless actually staged, is sufficient evidence of its dramatic nature. In the dialogue to which we have already referred, Professor Dobrée has much to say about the texture of dramatic dialogue, and pleads for a stage speech in which the changing speeds of the drama will be sensitively reflected—'a medium that can be at will swift, rhetorical or quiet . . . above all, a medium that shall be actor-proof, actor-easy, and clear, and which, though artificially made, shall sound on the stage as naturally rapid as the flowing of a stream'. The medium for dialogue would agree with this in many respects: it would, of course, be artificial, for all speech that is lifted out of the casualness of natural conversation into the formal arrangement of art is in that degree artificial; actors it will ignore; but it will be clear to express ideas, apt for repartee, and not so much swift as rhetorical, and not so much rhetorical as quiet. It is perhaps impossible to illustrate these qualities except in a complete dialogue, but the following passage from the opening of *Hylas and Philonous* is not wanting in the obvious texture of this kind of writing:

Phil. Good morning, Hylas: I did not expect to find you abroad so early.

Hyl. It is indeed something unusual; but my thoughts were so taken up with a subject I was discoursing of last night, that, finding I could not sleep, I resolved to rise and take a turn in the garden.

Phil. It happened well, to let you see what innocent and agreeable pleasures you lose every morning. Can there be a pleasanter time of the day, or a more delightful season of the year? That purple sky, those wild but sweet notes of birds, the fragrant bloom upon the trees and flowers, the gentle influence of the rising sun, these and a thousand nameless beauties of nature inspire the soul with secret transports; its faculties too, being at this time fresh and lively, are fit for these meditations, which the solitude of a garden and tranquillity of the morning naturally dispose us to. But I am afraid I interrupt your thoughts: for you seemed very intent on something.

Hyl. It is true, I was, and shall be obliged to you if you will permit me to go on in the same vein; not that I would by any means deprive myself of your company, for my thoughts always flow more easily in conversation with a friend than when I am alone: but my request is, that you would suffer me to impart my reflections to you.

Phil. With all my heart, it is what I should have requested myself if you had not prevented me.

Hyl. I was considering the odd fate of those men who have in all ages, through an affectation of being distinguished from the vulgar, or some unaccountable turn of thought, pretended either to believe nothing at all, or to believe the most extravagant things in the world. This however might be borne, if their paradoxes and scepticism did not draw after them some consequences of general disadvantage to mankind.

But the mischief lieth here; that when men of less leisure see them who are supposed to have spent their whole time in the pursuits of knowledge professing an entire ignorance of all things, or advancing such notions as are repugnant to plain and commonly received principles, they will be tempted to entertain suspicions concerning the most important truths, which they had hitherto held sacred and unquestionable.

Phil. I entirely agree with you, as to the ill tendency of the affected doubts of some philosophers, and fantastical conceits of others. I am even so far gone of late in this way of thinking, that I have quitted several of the sublime notions I had got in their schools for vulgar opinions. And I give it you on my word, since this revolt from metaphysical notions to the plain dictates of nature and common sense, I find my understanding strangely enlightened, so that I can now easily comprehend a great many things which before were all mystery and riddle.

Apart from the non-dramatic necessity, it is doubtful if any principle common to the three kinds of dialogue can be formulated. But it does remain to consider in what manner the three kinds fulfil their intentions. A platonic dialogue, such as the *Republic*, or such as Berkeley's *Alciphron*, proposes the logical establishment of a definite set of ideas; characters, imaginary, historical, or contemporary, are selected to personify points of view in relation to this body of ideas. Then the characters are 'set', and this 'setting' of the dialogue is not unimportant: it creates an attitude of sympathy towards the subject of discourse or even serves as a base of reference for the illustration of ideas. In the *Phaedo* we saw it used to effect distance: but its general use is to effect atmosphere, as in Dryden's masterly way, in *An Essay of Dramatic Poesy*. The scene of this dialogue is composed to perfection, giving stillness after tumult, a rhythm of oars, and a gradual passage into the sphere of abstractions:

It was that memorable day, in the first summer of the late war, when our navy engaged the Dutch; a day wherein the two most mighty and best appointed fleets which any age had ever seen, disputed the command of the greater part of the globe, the commerce of nations, and the riches of the universe. Whilst these vast floating bodies, on either side, moved against each other in parallel lines, and our countrymen under the happy conduct of his Royal Highness, went breaking, by little and little, into the line of the enemies; the noise of the cannon from both navies reached our ears about the City, so that all men being alarmed with it, and in a dreadful suspense of the event which we knew was then deciding, every one went following the sound as his fancy led him; and leaving the town almost empty, some took towards the park, some cross the river, others down it; all seeking the noise in the depth of silence.

Among the rest it was the fortune of Eugenius, Crites, Lisideius, and Neander, to be in company together; three of them persons whom their wit and quality have made known to all the town; and whom I have chose to hide under these borrowed names, that they may not suffer by so ill a relation as I am going to make of their discourse.

Taking then a barge which a servant of Lisideius had provided for them, they made haste to shoot the bridge, and left behind them that great fall of waters which hindered them from hearing what they desired; after which, having disengaged themselves from many vessels which rode at anchor in the Thames, and almost blocked up the passage towards Greenwich, they ordered the watermen to let fall their oars more gently; and then, every one favouring his own curiosity with a strict silence, it was not long ere they perceived the air break about them like the noise of distant thunder, or of swallows in a chimney: those little undulations of sound, though almost vanishing before they reached them, yet still seeming to retain somewhat of their first horror, which they had betwixt the fleets.

A dialogue that begins so naturally proceeds evenly; perhaps the convention of a scene may be kept up, as when Philonous stops to pluck a cherry and demonstrate that it is 'nothing but a congeries of sensible impressions', and usually a dialogue will end with some reversion to its setting, perhaps closing on a note of realism, as Dryden's does, with the party landing at the foot of Somerset Stairs and making their way 'through a crowd of French people, who were merrily dancing in the open air, and nothing concerned for the noise of guns which had alarmed the town that afternoon'.

The purpose of the dialogue is, we have contended, the expression of ideas; and a certain type of writer will resort to this form because it offers, as no other form can, the vivid presentation of opposing tenets. It must be confessed that some writers, without a mind on a subject, have thus used the form to expatiate on ideas which have no outcome. To be fair to both sides of a question is a laudable ambition, but it does not result in good literature. The vivid writer is the passionate one, even the prejudiced one; and the best dialogues of the expository kind lead to a decision. The logical proof is illustrated by the defeat in argument of the opponents of the thesis; and the resulting effect on the reader is ever so much more exhilarating than if he had merely read through a direct exposition. For one thing, rhetoric comes naturally at the crisis of an argument, and rhetoric in a due place will yield a heightened beauty of expression and a fine force of effect. For this reason the *Essay of Dramatic Poesy* is justly held to be the finest example of Dryden's prose; and it is impossible to insist too strongly on the pure literary quality of *Hylas and Philonous* and of *Alciphron*. Under the influence of the form of the dialogue, Berkeley's style, almost the purest and serenest in English literature, takes on an unrivalled precision and beauty.

The quality of the second (which is Lucian's) kind of dialogue is rather indefinable, and is best approached by a quotation from Diderot's *Rêve de D'Alembert*:

> *Mademoiselle de l'Espinasse.* . . . Docteur, qu'est-ce que c'est que le sophisme de l'éphémère?
> *Bordeu.* C'est celui d'un être passager qui croît à l'immortalité des choses.
> *Mademoiselle de l'Espinasse.* La rose de Fontenelle qui disait que de mémoire de rose on n'avait vu mourir un jardinier?
> *Bordeu.* Précisément; cela est léger et profond.

Léger et profond! It is the secret of all art. We are reminded of Nietzsche's emphatic phrase: What is good is easy; everything divine runs with light feet.

It is this secret that perpetuates the charm of Lucian and of his later reincarnation, Bernard de Fontenelle. Not that Lucian and Fontenelle have much in common, apart from their secret. Lucian's method is gay ridicule, with nothing beyond but sanity and sensible worldliness. This 'last great master of Attic eloquence and Attic wit' gave to the dialogue variety, but not a little at the expense of its dignity. Lucian was one of those destructive spirits whose only weapon is irony; he was, in addition, a rhetorician, practised in the elaboration of fictitious 'cases', and when he came to use the dialogue, he found his qualities conjoining happily in this literary form. The dialogue enabled him to express that detachment of observation essential to irony and it enabled him to present, almost dramatically, it must be confessed, the opposition of equal absurdities. Irony is the weapon of a second-rate writer, but it is not without its uses. It can demolish absurdities, pomposities and vanities; and it can amuse an audience. Lucian is still very good reading and he exists in an English translation which is itself a work of bounteous wit.[1] These translators have observed, in their introduction, that Lucian did not leave the dialogue as he found it; he profoundly modified its form. Beginning with an almost Platonic use, he only gradually came to a satiric use.

That was an idea that we may suppose to have occurred to him after the composition of the 'Hermotimus'. This is in form the most philosophic of his dialogues. . . . The dialogue that, perhaps, comes next,

[1] *The Works of Lucian of Samosata* translated by H. W. Fowler and F. G. Fowler. Four volumes Oxford (Clarendon Press) 1905

'The Parasite', is still Platonic in form, but only as a parody; its main interest . . . is in the combination for the first time of satire with dialogue. One more step remained to be taken. . . . It was the fusing of Comedy and Dialogue—the latter being the prose conversation that had hitherto been confined to philosophical discussion. The new literary form, then, was conversation, frankly for purposes of entertainment, as in Comedy, but to be read and not acted.

This brings us back to technical distinctions. It is an exact description of Lucian's method and reveals what, on any strict regard for the purity of the form, we must consider as his weakness. For in adopting his conversational tone Lucian deliberately abandoned the artifice of art. Conversation to be read (not acted) is really a contradiction in terms; at any rate, it is a confusion of terms. Conversation has its place in naturalistic narrative, but as a *literary* means it does not rightly exist. From the same confusion all 'conversational' criteria of prose style break down: art, it can never be too often repeated, is discipline, definiteness, abstraction from chaos. Conversation is liberal, easy, redundant, organically natural; and the art that apes conversation partakes of its formless qualities.

It is the distinction of Fontenelle that, while following Lucian in the variety and subtlety of his particular method, he yet contrived to give his dialogues a texture of stylistic dignity and to endow them with intellectual complexity. Lucian, for all his gifts, tends to be a little banal. Not so Fontenelle. He is an obscure and enticing author, attracting the sympathetic mind to strong affections and irrational

loyalty. His calm intelligence, equally devoid of
enthusiasms and prejudices, perhaps came naturally
and of necessity to this only perfectly detached form
of writing. The form was made for a man of his
temperament—not poet, not scientist, but *homme
de lettres*, a subtle spirit standing between the worlds
of knowledge and sensibility. His intellectual graces
give him a certain solidity which is lacking in Lucian,
and this he has without any loss of wit. In this
solidity is his main distinction; but instead of the
anomalous word 'solidity' we might venture on 'purpose'. 'Tous vos Dialogues', he writes in his dedication of the *Nouveaux Dialogues des Morts* to Lucian
('aux Champs Elisiens'), 'renferment leur moral, et
j'ay fait moraliser tous mes Morts; autrement ce
n'eût pas esté la peine de les faire parler ; des Vivans
auroient suffi pour dire des choses inutiles'. In the
same place Fontenelle, writing of Lucian's style,
distinguishes 'cette simplicité fine, et cet enjouement
naïf, qui sont si propres pour le Dialogue'—thus
showing his deliberate conception of the form.
Lucian had purpose too, as Fontenelle says, but it is
merely the moral purpose of the leveller and satirist.
Fontenelle himself had more, for he had a positive
intellectual aim. He is the exponent of Descartes
and Leibniz, and by giving a literary flavour to the
new 'experimental philosophy' (a term which he invented), he became, in Faguet's neat phrase, 'le père
discret et prudent' of the whole eighteenth century.

It was left to Landor to elaborate the third kind
of dialogue. *Imaginary Conversations* is not an idle
synonym for 'Dialogues', but describes more pre-

cisely the nature of the adopted *genre*. Landor was a classical writer in a romantic age, but he could not quite escape the influence of his environment. You can get a very exact contrast between his and Fontenelle's method by comparing *The Maid of Orleans and Agnes Sorel* with *Agnès Sorel et Roxelane*. Both writers proposed to illustrate the same theme—the influence of women on the affairs of men—and both selected Agnes Sorel as an embodiment of the idea. In Fontenelle's dialogue Agnes and Roxelane discuss the subject, illustrating it from their own experiences, and the moral of the dialogue is driven home in the climax of the argument:

> *A. Sorel.* J'avoue qu'il est beau d'assujettir ceux qui se précautionnent tant contre notre pouvoir.
>
> *Roxelane.* Les hommes ont beau faire; quand on les prend par les passions, on les mène où l'on veut. Qu'on me fasse revivre, et qu'on me donne l'Homme du monde le plus impérieux; je feray de luy tout ce qu'il me plaira, pourveu que j'aye beaucoup d'esprit, assez de beauté, & peu d'amour.

Landor's procedure is very different. He seizes on the romantic legend of Jeanne d'Arc's pleading with Agnes to use her love to awaken the King's latent patriotism; and he puts this scene, in all but rubrics into dramatic form:

> *Jeanne.* I am so ignorant, I know only a part of my duties; yet those which my Maker has taught me I am earnest to perform. He teaches me that divine love has less influence over the heart than human; he teaches me that it ought to have more: finally, he commands me to announce to thee, not his anger, but his will.

Agnes. Declare it; O declare it. I do believe his holy word is deposited in thy bosom.

Jeanne. Encourage the king to lead his vassals to the field.

Agnes. When the season is milder.

Jeanne. And bid him leave you for ever.

Agnes. Leave me! one whole campaign! one entire summer! Oh anguish! It sounded in my ears as if you had said 'for ever'.

Jeanne. I say it again.

Agnes. Thy power is superhuman, mine is not.

Jeanne. It ought to be, in setting God at defiance. The mightiest of the angels rued it.

Agnes. We did not make our hearts.

Jeanne. But we can mend them.

Agnes. Oh! mine (God knows it) bleeds.

Jeanne. Say rather it expels from it the last stagnant drop of its rebellious sin. Salutary pangs may be painfuller than mortal ones.

Agnes. Bid him leave me! wish it! permit it! think it near! believe it ever can be! Go, go . . . I am lost eternally.

Apart from the Landorian phrasing, which is fashioned and beautiful, the method is naturalistic, evocative of the sentimental associations of the scene. In Landor's case the theme is staged, in Fontenelle's it is stated, with precision and an effect of finality. Landor's method is the freshest, the least exploited, the most lavish in its possibilites. And for these reasons it is likely to find the more practicians in the future. But it has its limitations, the greatest of which is confusion with dramatic form. The fear is that the 'imaginary conversation' will merely dissipate on miniature drama energy that might be guided into more effective channels. For surrounding this later form, merging with its circumference, is the waste, the wilderness of anecdote.

Lucian's method is personal and must wait for a wit born to the manner; but the Platonic form is there for anyone with taste, intelligence and ideas. It shows all its suppleness, its beauty and its philosophic grace in a dialogue of our own time the *Eupalinos* of Paul Valéry,[1] In this exquisite dialogue —curiously comparable in its subject-matter with the third dialogue of *Alciphron*—we get the use of that technical device already discovered by Plato and subsequently developed by Lucian and Diderot,[2] in which the unity of a dialogue is preserved but the number of points of view conveniently increased by the introduction of dialogue within dialogue—that is, a dialogue reported by one of the speakers. It is a detail, but another device used by Valéry in *L'Ame et la Danse* (the companion dialogue to *Eupalinos*) is of great beauty and of unmatched subtlety. The speakers are represented witnessing a Greek dancer, and as they watch, discussing the nature of the soul, the dance, in its movement and its music, becomes a symbol of the soul, and as the dance 'works out' so does the argument. It is a perfect union of thought and action, so intimately interlinked that there is no question of the dramatic fallacy—the drama is an enduring metaphor; the action is in the ideas.

[1] Paul Valéry *Eupalinos, ou L'Architecte*, précédé de *L'Ame et la Danse* Paris 1923

[2] And by Juvenal, in a solitary example (Satire IX). But this dialogue is in verse, a complication I have deliberately avoided in this essay.

7

POETRY AND EXPERIENCE

AN alternative title for this essay might be 'Memory and Emotion' for it will circle round Wordsworth's famous definition of poetry as 'emotion recollected in tranquillity' (with its important rider that the emotion so recollected 'is contemplated till, by a species of re-action, the tranquillity gradually disappears, and an emotion, *kindred to that which was before the subject of contemplation*, is *gradually* produced and does itself *actually exist* in the mind'). It is not my wish to enlarge on this definition, or comment on the psychological subtlety implied by the phrases I have italicized; that has been done recently and with great perceptiveness by Mr. Christopher Salvesen.[1] For many years it has been my conviction that Wordsworth, 'aided and abetted' by Coleridge, had expressed the final truth about the nature of the poetic process, and everything that has been written on the subject since his time, including Poe's essay and Paul Valéry's commentary and *approfondissement* of that essay, has affirmed but not essentially modified Wordsworth's theory. As that theory is wholly psychological we might expect, and do

[1] Christopher Salvesen *The Landscape of Memory* Edward Arnold, London 1965

indeed find, that modern psychological speculations, especially those of Freud and Jung, have given us some further understanding of the *dynamics* of the process. We can now give a more precise explanation of what Wordsworth was content to call 'a species of re-action'; and Schachtel, in the important essay which I shall quote at length on a later page, has shown us in what precise sense memory functions as a dynamic force in poetic expression. Indeed, though Dr. Schachtel never mentions Wordsworth's famous preface of 1800, his own essay *On Memory and Childhood Amnesia* is a re-statement of Wordsworth's theory of inspiration in terms of modern psychology.

My present purpose is to enquire more closely into one aspect of the theory not discussed either by Wordsworth, Coleridge or Schachtel—namely, the nature of the experience that causes the emotion that is afterwards recollected or recalled. What is an experience, and is there a special kind of emotion, aroused by a special kind of experience that calls for poetic expression? Does any kind of experience give rise to an emotion that is a fit subject for creative recall? Is every kind of emotion a fit subject for poetry?

These questions have been suggested to me by long meditation on a particular kind of experience and its expression in the poetry of my own time—the experience of war. Perhaps I should be more specific and for war in general substitute 'modern warfare', though the difference is perhaps only one of degree (but can we in any meaningful way compare Troy and Hiroshima?). I have thought about this subject for the very good reason that as a young poet I was myself involved in war and challenged to write about war, both as an actuality and as a memory. A problem existed and it began to be publicly debated when in 1936 Yeats edited *The Oxford Book of Modern Verse* and excluded the poetry of the actual experience of war written by Wilfred Owen, Siegfried Sassoon and others. He chose instead a poem of my own based on war emotions 'recollected in tranquillity'.

Yeats's decision, which aroused bitter resentment, has been much misunderstood, and hitherto I have refrained from commenting on it because as a poet who had been preferred I was too obviously an interested party. But now, many years after the event, I feel I can review the problem dispassionately enough, and since it is a problem much wider than the occasion that provoked the outcry against Yeats, it can perhaps be lifted on to a more philosophical plane.

Apart from the poem chosen by Yeats and written about fifteen years after the end of the First World War, I wrote other poems under the immediate impact of my war experience, and these also stand condemned by Yeats's criterion. If I accept Yeats's reasoning I must reject the poetic worth of these few poems. *Fiat justitia!*

If I try to recall the circumstances under which I wrote these immediate or 'actual' poems, it was always a sight seen or an event experienced that aroused my emotions, and during that state of excitement I began composition. The recent event did 'actually exist in the mind', but there was no significant 'distance' between the mind and the event. Yeats calls this state of mind 'withdrawing into the quicksilver at the back of the mirror, where no great event becomes luminous in the poet's mind', and by this I assume he meant that the poet identifies the self with the reflected image.

The image in question, if not in scientific terminology 'eidetic', is still sensational (i.e. it has the immediacy of a perceptual image). What is absent is a sense of time, and of the 'screen' that time interposes between experience and recollection.

Poetry should be vivid—word should match image and the image should be 'concrete', the natural object itself. Why then should time or duration have any importance in the process of poetic creation? The answer would seem to lie in certain phenomena to which we give the names infinity and universality. Infinity is an aspect of time, universality an aspect of place. What is infinite is time that has no beginning and no end, but yet is not timeless; and what is universal is place or extension that has no beginning and no end and yet has existence. It would seem—this was certainly Wordsworth's belief and I think we may assume that it was also Yeats's belief—that the quality of poetry is in some way associated with those vague but indispensable concepts of time and place.

Against such an attitude in poetic theory and practice we have the whole school of realists, who believe that art can dispense not only with infinity and universality (which they condemn as metaphysical concepts) but also with memory (which they condemn as nostalgia). Poetry like certain brands of coffee is 'instant', the direct expression of a spontaneous emotion—Lawrence was very conscious of this contrast: 'Eternity is only an abstraction from the actual present. Infinity is only a great reservoir of recollection, or a reservoir of aspiration: man-made. The quivering nimble hour of the present, this is the quick of Time. This is the immanence. The quick of the universe is the *pulsating, carnal self*, mysterious and palpable.'[1]

One answer to this problem is to dismiss it as irrelevant and re-assert Mallarmé's definition—poetry is made of *words*. This is often called the magical theory of poetry, but it is not a theory of the creative process but rather a description of poetic substance: the words are magical, but we must still seek the force that produces them and makes them magical.

According to Lawrence, this force is the directness of the utterance itself, 'the insurgent naked throb of the instant moment'. But if we look at Lawrence's own most immediate poems, such as those published in *Look! We Have Come Through* (1917), which in a foreword he described as 'an essential story, or history, or confession, unfolding one from the other in organic development, the whole revealing the intrinsic experience of a man during the crisis of manhood, when he marries and comes into himself', we find passion and sincerity, utterance 'like a spasm', but no magic, only the clichés of naked sentimentality, too embarrassing to quote.

Instead I shall quote from two war poems:

[1] Introduction to the American edition of *New Poems* 1920 *Phoenix* 1936 p 220

1 If in some smothering dreams you too could pace
  Behind the waggon that we flung him in,
  And watch the white eyes writhing in his face,
  His hanging face, like a devil's sick of sin;
  If you could hear, at every jolt, the blood
  Come gurgling from the froth-corrupted lungs,
  Obscene as cancer, bitter as the cud
  Of vile, incurable sores on innocent tongues,
  My friend, you would not tell with such high zest
  To children ardent for some desperate glory,
  The old lie: Dulce et decorum est
  Pro patria mori.

2 His wild heart beats with painful sobs,
  His strained hands clench an ice-cold rifle,
  His aching jaws grip a hot parched tongue,
  And his wide eyes search unconsciously.

  He cannot shriek
  Bloody saliva
  Dribbles down his shapeless jacket

  I saw him stab
  And stab again
  A well-killed Boche

  This is the happy warrior,
  This is he. . . .

The first extract is from *Dulce Et Decorum Est*, one of Wilfred Owen's poems; the second is from one of my own poems and I include it only to implicate myself as well as Owen in the observations I am going to make.

Both poems describe passive suffering and Yeats's charge, based on Matthew Arnold, is that 'passive suffering is not a theme for poetry'. Arnold held strongly—it was the main theme of the 1853 preface to his poems, that in poetry 'all depends upon the subject; choose a fitting action . . . everything else will follow'. A fitting subject must be positive, vital, life-enhancing, qualities to which Arnold gave the somewhat ambiguous name 'interpretative':

> The grand power of poetry is its interpretative power; by which I mean, not a power of drawing out in black and white an explanation of the mystery of the universe, but the power of so dealing with things as to awaken in us a wonderfully full, new, and intimate sense of them, and of our relations with them. When this sense is awakened in us, as to objects without us, we feel ourselves to be in contact with the essential nature of those objects, to be no longer bewildered and oppressed by them, but to have their secret, and to be in harmony with them; and this feeling calms and satisfies us as no other can.[1]

It is true that in the same essay Arnold distinguishes between the 'natural magic' of poetry and its 'moral profundity'; it 'interprets' in two ways: 'It interprets by expressing with magical felicity the physiognomy and movement of the outward world, and it interprets by expressing, with inspired conviction, the ideas and laws of the inward world of man's moral and spiritual nature'. Natural magic is the quality we all desire to give and to receive in poetry, but moral profundity, for which we might easily substitute the phrase 'moral realism' to make it more acceptable to our own age, is another question. How does the poet introduce moral realism into his poetry? By choosing a fit theme, we are told. Why then is not passive suffering a fit theme?

[1] Matthew Arnold. Essay on 'Maurice de Guérin' *Essays in Criticism* 1865

It will not do to suggest as I (and presumably Yeats) have done, that the depiction of passive suffering does not have the power of so dealing with things as to awaken in us a wonderfully full, new, and intimate sense of them, and of our relations with them. In Owen's poem the image of the gassed soldier gives us a very intimate sense of 'things', of 'objects without us'; but, Arnold would ask, do we then understand the essential nature of these objects (yes, we may still answer), and 'to be no longer bewildered and oppressed by them' (here we hesitate to assent: we are desperately bewildered by the obscene sight, which contradicts our traditional belief that it is sweet and noble to die for one's country. And when Arnold probes further to ask us whether we have the secret of this action, and feel in harmony with it, we retreat in horrified dissent, neither calm nor satisfied by the poet's interpretation).

It is an interruption, but we might ask whether a pictorial interpretation of the same scene could possibly satisfy us by its 'natural magic' and 'moral profundity'. There were such interpretations of events in the First World War, most of them German, strictly comparable to Owen's poem; the best known are the paintings of Otto Dix and Georg Gross. These are strict witnesses to the reality of that war, as any survivor can testify; but we cannot contemplate them as works of art. They inspire feelings of anger and disgust, and we hide them away in the cellars of some war museum.

'All a poet can do today is warn', wrote Owen in the preface to his poems, and in these words he resigned the interpretative function of poetry. When he said 'the Poetry is in the pity' he implied that it was not where it should be, in a magical felicity expressing the physiognomy and movement of the outward world. Owen sacrificed felicity and harmony (the proper ingredients of poetry) for Truth, the truth about war. It may be argued that the sacrifice was worth while, that Truth is more important than Beauty. But Arnold's point is that Truth and Beauty must be reconciled in poetry—to give man 'a satisfying sense of reality'; to reconcile man with himself and the universe.

For Homer, and for all poets since Homer until perhaps Tennyson, it was still possible to find a fit subject in war, or at least in certain aspects of war—courage, or comradeship, for example. But as Yeats said 'it is no longer possible to write *The Persians, Agincourt, Chevy Chase*: some blunderer has driven his car on to the wrong side of the road'. During the Second World War I tried to express the same truth in these lines:

> The kind of war is chang'd: the crusade heart
> out-shatter'd: flesh a stain on broken earth
> and death an unresisted rain.
> The horror loos'd all honour is lost.
> Peace has pride and passion; but no evil
> to equal the indignity of war, whose ringing anvil
> wins only anguish. The weighted hammer
> breaks the stretch'd tendons at the wrist
> and leaves the soul a twisted nail
> tearing the flesh that still would live
> and give to words the brutal edge of truth.

But the edge of truth is not necessarily brutal; I ought to have used a word that implied that intimate sense of final harmony in things. With Arnold 'I will not now inquire whether this sense is illusive, whether it does absolutely make us possess the real nature of things; all I say is, that poetry can awaken it in us, and that to awaken it is one of the highest powers of poetry'.

But how? To aim consciously at 'moral profundity' is a fatal temptation in the poet, and Arnold himself too often succumbed to it. *Empedocles on Etna* is but one self-confessed example of it:

> Slave of sense
> I have in no wise been; but slave of thought?

He was fully aware of the danger and in a letter to his sister, Mrs. Foster, probably of 1849, wrote: 'More and more I feel bent against the modern English habit (too much encouraged by Wordsworth) of using poetry for thinking aloud, instead of making anything'. Hopkins called the lowest kind of poetry 'poetical language'. 'To use that, which poetasters, and indeed almost everyone, can do, is not more necessarily to be uttering poetry than striking the keys of a piano is playing a tune.' A little higher than this kind is Parnassian. 'Can only be used by real poets. Can be written without inspiration . . . Common in professedly descriptive pieces. Much of it in *Paradise Lost* and *Regained*. Nearly all *The Faery Queen*.'[1] On another occasion he could scarcely point anywhere to anything more idiomatically Parnassian than Tennyson's *Enoch Arden*, and 'no author palls so much as Wordsworth; this is because he

[1] *Notebooks and Papers of Gerard Manley Hopkins*. Edited by Humphrey House. Oxford 1937 p 29

H

writes such an "intolerable deal of" Parnassian'. He also, Hopkins admits, writes 'a higher sort of Parnassian which I call *Castalian*' which is 'too characteristic of the poet, too so-and-so-all-over-ish, to be quite inspiration.' E.g.

> Yet despair
> Touches me not, though pensive as a bird
> Whose vernal coverts winter hath laid bare.

This is 'too essentially Wordsworth, too persistently his way of looking at things'. The only genuine poetry is the poetry of inspiration (later we have called it 'pure poetry') and this Hopkins defines as 'a mood of great, abnormal in fact, mental acuteness, either energetic or receptive, according as thoughts which arise in it seem generated by a stress and action of the brain, or to strike into it unasked. This mood arises from various causes, physical generally, as good health or state of the air, or prosaic as it is, length of time after a meal'.[1]

It might be argued that Arnold's division of poets into 'slaves of sense' and 'slaves of thought', does not exhaust the possibilities of poetic servitude. The modern poet tends to be a slave to something more insidious, which undoubtedly comes under Hopkins's condemnation of 'using poetry for thinking aloud, instead of making anything'. Wordsworth, given as an example by Hopkins, certainly did a lot of thinking aloud, especially in his later verse—thinking aloud about liberty and order (one sonnet is entitled *Com-*

---

[1] The quotations in this paragraph come from a letter to Alexander William Mowbray Baillie dated 10 September 1864 *Further Letters of Gerard Manley Hopkins*, edited by C. C. Abbott. Oxford 1956 pp 215-23

posed after reading a Newspaper of the Day and reads like it), thinking aloud about celebrated events in ancient and contemporary history, thinking aloud about the doctrines of the Church of England, thinking aloud about the Reform Bill or the Projected Kendal and Windermere Railway (what a hero he would have made of Dr. Beeching!). These are, of course, serious subjects, worthy of thought; we are sometimes interested to have Wordsworth's ideas on the questions of his day, and his High Toryism was motivated by lofty ideals and not, like the Low Toryism of our own time, by thoughts of profits and dividends. But it is not the substance of the thought that Hopkins complained about, but the mental process itself, which is foreign to any state of mind which we may call inspirational. Such a critical consideration must be applied to all the verse in our own time that would justify itself by a claim of social relevance. The unfortunate poets of communist régimes are the worst offenders, but at least they have the excuse of 'force majeure'; to revolt in the name of pure poetry, as Pasternak did, requires immense personal courage and may be of no avail. But the poets of England and North America do not have this excuse: they write uninspired verse about uninspiring subjects because nothing else 'happens' to them, nothing else is *seen* by them. I do not really need to give you an example of this 'thinking aloud', which is almost universal in contemporary verse. The attitude is beautifully satirized in a poem by the American writer, E. B. White, *I paint what I see*:

> I paint what I paint, I paint what I see,
>   I paint what I think, said Rivera,

And the thing that is dearest in life to me
In a bourgeois hall is Integrity;
>   However. . . .
I'll take out a couple of people drinkin'
And put in a picture of Abraham Lincoln,
I could even give you McCormick's reaper
And still not make my art much cheaper.
But the head of Lenin has got to stay
Or my friends will give me the bird today
>   The bird, the bird, forever.

More seriously, the integrity of poetry, its independence of social problems and practical concerns, finds its perfect defence in Yeats's poem, *Lapis Lazuli*, which is a parable illustrating the truths he expressed more prosaically and more gnomically in the Introduction to *The Oxford Book of Modern Verse*. I quote its conclusion:

>   Two Chinamen, behind them a third,
>   Are carved in lapis lazuli,
>   Over them flies a long-legged bird,
>   A symbol of longevity;
>   The third, doubtless a serving man,
>   Carries a musical instrument.
>
>   Every discoloration of the stone,
>   Every accidental crack or dent,
>   Seems a water-course or an avalanche,
>   Or lofty slope where it still snows
>   Though doubtless plum or cherry-branch
>   Sweetens the little half-way house
>   Those Chinamen climb towards, and I
>   Delight to imagine them seated there;
>   There, on the mountain and the sky,
>   On all the tragic scene they stare.

One asks for mournful melodies;
Accomplished fingers begin to play.
Their eyes mid many wrinkles, their eyes,
Their ancient, glittering eyes, are gay.

It may be that the mood of inspiration, as described by Hopkins, is more intense than the divine indifference depicted by Yeats, but one is describing the nature of poetry and the other its social purpose. Hopkins is telling us how poetry is made; Yeats is telling us that poetry has no power to transform society:

Though Hamlet rambles and Lear rages,
And all the drop-scenes drop at once
Upon a hundred thousand stages,
It cannot grow by an inch or an ounce.

We may ask what then is the relation of the highest kind of poetry to experience, and if, as I do, we accept the views of Hopkins and Yeats, we must conclude that the relationship can only be indirect. The thoughts which *arise* in a state of inspiration arise from some hidden source, not from direct perception or observation. They may be generated by 'a stress and action of the brain' (an effort of recollection in Wordsworth's sense) or they 'strike into it unasked'. What is quite certain is that they are not descriptive or discursive. They do not proceed in a logical sequence determined by a conscious purpose.

Nevertheless, as Hopkins would have been the first to admit, meditative verse can be a poetry of inspiration, and there is no better example of it than Wordsworth's *Ode: Intimations of Immortality*. We know from his own statement that Wordsworth wrote the first four stanzas in one burst of inspiration, and then waited 'two years at least' before he was inspired to write the continuation. The poem is obscure and critics have complained that it is illogical; nevertheless, it is pure poetry of the most essential kind. Hopkins thought that 'St. George and St. Thomas of Canterbury wore roses in heaven for England's sake on the day that ode, not without intercession, was penned'. 'There have been in history', he wrote in the same letter to Canon Dixon, 'a few, a very few men, whom common repute, even where it did not trust them, has treated as having had something happen to them that does not happen to other men, as having *seen something*, whatever that really was. Plato is the most famous of these . . . human nature in these men saw something, got a shock; wavers in opinion, looking back, whether there was anything in it or no; but is in a tremble ever since. Now what Wordsworthians mean is . . . that in Wordsworth when he wrote that Ode human nature got another of those shocks, and the tremble from it is spreading. This opinion I do strongly share; I am, ever since I knew the ode, in that tremble'.[1]

The experience of poetry is in the act of creation: the experience is the poetry and is a wholly mental event. Experience in the external sense, as an immediate perceptual experience, has withdrawn into the quicksilver at the back of the mirror and is no longer luminous. The best that the poet can do with experience in this sense is to bury it. In the unconscious mind it may strike roots; from that hidden

[1] *The Correspondence of Gerard Manley Hopkins and Richard Watson Dixon* edited by C. C. Abbott. Oxford 1935 pp 147-8

source it may send up a shoot, strike into the conscious brain 'unasked', and then the poet receives a shock, *sees* something with mental acuteness and describes what he sees in words that have a 'natural magic'.

8

THE RESURRECTION OF THE WORD

A PROBLEM exists for the modern poet (in which term I include all who use language as a symbolic process) which Mallarmé was the first to formulate and attempt to overcome—the evident fact that the language of our western civilization had become too corrupt for poetic use. Corruption is perhaps not quite the exact word to describe a state of exhaustion or evisceration, and the consequential resort, in any process of verbalization, to the cliché.

That this is a problem affecting not only the poet, but social communication in general, has been the concern of one of the most perceptive of modern psychologists, Ernest G. Schachtel, and in this essay I shall take advantage of his formulation of the general problem.

Schachtel's essays on the subject are now collected in a volume called *Metamorphosis: On the Development of Affect, Perception, Attention and Memory*.[1] The most relevant of these essays is the one on *Memory and Childhood Amnesia*, originally published in *Psychiatry* in 1947; it has been reprinted

[1] Basic Books, New York 1959

several times and I have more than once called attention to its bearing on the problems of poetic criticism. This essay seeks to explain how and why 'in the course of later childhood, adolescence and adult life, perception and experience themselves develop increasingly into the rubber stamps of conventional clichés. The capacity to see and feel what is there gives way to the tendency to see and feel what one expects to see and feel, which, in turn, is what one is expected to see and feel because everybody else does'. Experience is pre-digested, as it were, and people 'turn the potential nourishment of the anticipated experience into the sterile currency of the conventional phrase which exhausts their experience because they have seen, heard, felt nothing but this phrase with which later they will report to their friends the "exciting time" they have had'. Art, according to Dr. Schachtel, is the heroic attempt to escape from such a schematization of experience. 'It is in those experiences which transcend the cultural schemata, in those memories of experience which transcend the conventional memory schemata, that every new insight and every true work of art has its origin, and that the hope of progress, of a widening of the scope of human endeavour and human life, is founded.'

That is Dr. Schachtel's thesis, as it relates to art in general, but I may perhaps be excused another quotation from an equally relevant essay on *Secondary Autocentricity*. For the meaning of such terms as auto- and allocentricity I must refer the reader to the book itself, but throughout his work Dr. Schachtel makes use of a distinction between autocentric, i.e. subject-centred, and allocentric, i.e. object-centred, modes of perception. 'In the autocentric mode there is little or no objectification; the emphasis is on how and what the person feels, there is a close relation, amounting to a fusion, between sensory quality and pleasure or unpleasure feelings, and the perceiver reacts primarily to something impinging on him. . . . In the allocentric mode there is objectification, the emphasis is on what the object is like; there is either no relation or a less pronounced or less direct relation between perceived sensory qualities and pleasure-unpleasure feelings—that is, such feelings are usually absent or less pronounced or of a different quality; the perceiver usually approaches or turns to the object actively and in doing so either opens himself towards it receptively or, figuratively or literally, takes hold of it, tries to "grasp" it.'

We are now prepared for the passage from Dr. Schachtel's book most relevant to my immediate purpose:

'*Language* itself . . . imparts certain viewpoints which can help or hinder the development of allocentric perception, can open or obscure the world. The word, of course, never can take the place of the object or the quality or the activity which it designates or indicates. But most of the time, when we listen to the spoken or read the written word, we neither perceive nor imagine the referent of the word but are in contact only with the words (or concepts). We behave as if the word were really all there is to the object which it designates. The label (sign) becomes a substitute for its referent, and thus, in listening or reading we are divorced from any experience of that which the words point to. More often than not, the speaker or writer who uses these words is also in contact only with them and not with the objects they designate. Used in this way language bars the access to the world, obscures the objects, leads to autocentric perception of familiar clichés rather than to allocentric perception of reality. On the opposite pole, language can be evocative of experience. The evocative function of language depends usually on the speaker's (or writer's) being in contact with the experience about which he speaks and trying to communicate (i.e. evoke in the listener) this experience, and on the listener's willingness and ability to experience (rather than just hearing words) what is being said to him. The way in which language is used can have a decisive influence on whether experimental communication takes place in which both people (speaker and listener, writer and reader) are in touch with the referent of the communication, or whether only words are exchanged and no experience is evoked. The evocative function of the language can be enhanced by avoiding clichés and by lifting words out of their most banal, current use and using them in a way that reveals their original meaning, or by using them in such combinations, images, positions as will conjure up most concretely the experience about which one is talking or writing. Good writers and poets excel in evocative use of lanuage; in our day they often have to shock the reader out of the state of mind in which he is capable only of taking in clichés and is blind to experience. I believe that this necessity accounts for much of the seeming obscurity of modern poetry and literature. With the invention of printing and with the constant assault of the modern mass-communication media, language has lost a great deal of its evocative function and the listener or reader merely takes in clichés, which altogether too often is all that the speaker or writer, on his part, was in touch with.'

One further short quotation from the same essay: 'In its origins language is always evocative. If we take the pains really to fathom a word, even the most worn one will become pregnant with meaning, the word misused in the most banal cliché will again become evocative of experience. *Really listening to the word* and all its implications can accomplish such resurrection of its experimental meaning buried under layers of daily use, and very often a tracing of the history of the word, back to its earliest roots, will recover its evocative impact.'

In the passages I have quoted (and elsewhere in his deeply significant work) Dr. Schachtel is giving scientific formulation to the predicament of modern poetry that Mallarmé was the first to reveal. I do not deliberately ignore the possible priority of Rimbaud, but there is no question of influence. Most of Rimbaud's miraculous poems were written in the years 1870-72, but Mallarmé does not seem to have become acquainted with his work until Verlaine quoted some verses in the course of an article published in 1883, by which year Mallarmé was already forty-one and had written his most characteristic verse—*L'Après-midi d'un Faune*, for example, was written in 1865. Mallarmé's final, poetically revolutionary poem, *Un Coup de Dés jamais n'abolira le Hasard*, was not composed until 1897. Rimbaud's 'long, immense et raisonné *dérèglement* de *tous les sens*' only incidentally involved the word, though lines like

Un hydrolat lacrymal lave
Les cieux vert-chou. . . .

point the way; and *Les Illuminations* (1872) is a collection of 'neo-narratives'. *Les Chants de Maldoror* were composed by Isidore Ducasse a few years earlier, between 1867 and 1870 (when he died), a fantastic case of synchronicity. The world was ready for a resurrection of the word.

These historical questions are perhaps irrelevant; all I wish to establish is that poets were already aware, before the end of the last century, of the poetic bankruptcy of *language itself*. Between 1886 and 1896 Mallarmé wrote various articles from which he later assembled a series of notes to which he gave the title *Crise de Vers*. It is reprinted in *Oeuvres Complètes*.[1] In these notes Mallarmé announces the possibility of a renewal of poetry through the musical modulation of words, a 'pure' poetry as he called it. Such a pure poetry would require the disappearance of the poet himself, in so far as he has the pretension to express a self; the initiative passes to the words mobilized to shock by their diversity—words that illuminate each other reciprocally as if a fuse of sparks flashed from gem to gem, substituting for a perceptible breathing the divine afflatus or the inspired energy of the phrase itself. (Mallarmé's prose is almost more difficult to translate than his verse, but I think I am faithful to his meaning.) He writes of the inescapable need of his time to separate, as if for different purposes, the double function of the word, one *'brut ou immédiat*

[1] Bibliothèque de la Pléiade, Paris 1945 pp 360-8

(i.e. allocentric), the other essential (i.e. autocentric). Still more precisely Mallarmé suggests that a verse which from several syllables *(vocables)* makes up a new 'total' word, foreign to the language and incantatory in effect, achieves the isolation of the word. At the same time it eliminates the element of chance that clings to terms despite the re-tempering they undergo by being steeped alternately in sense and sound. Hence the surprise of never having heard a phrase or fragment of speech succeed in evoking the object itself, at the same time bathing it in a new atmosphere—in Schachtel's words, lifting the words out of their most banal, current use to reveal their original meaning and conjure up the concreteness of the experience one is writing about.

Paul Valéry, who was a direct disciple of Mallarmé, throws further light on this poetic revolution, which he defines as 'an effort by one man to create an artificial ideal order by means of a material of vulgar origin'. In his essay on *Pure Poetry* (actually notes for a lecture[1]) he defines the problem of pure poetry in this way: 'whether one can make a whole work out of these elements, so recognizable, so distinct from those of the language I have called *insensible*; and consequently whether by means of a work, in verse or not, one can give the impression of a complete system of *reciprocal* relations between our ideas and images on the one hand and our means of expression on the other—a system which would correspond particularly to the creation of an emotive

[1] Translated by Denise Folliot in *The Art of Poetry* vol 7 in *The Collected Works of Paul Valéry* Bollingen Series, New York 1958 pp 184-92

state of mind'. It is not my intention to contribute to the discussion of 'pure poetry', a concept which originated in France and which has usually, in English criticism, been pursued on a depressingly superficial level. But as Valéry says, 'instead of *pure poetry* it would perhaps be better to say *absolute poetry*, and it should then be understood in the sense of a search for the effects resulting from the relations between words, or rather the relations of the overtones of words among themselves, which suggests, in short, *an exploration of that whole domain of sensibility which is governed by language*'. The italics are Valéry's but the phrase will serve to describe the purpose of certain experimental writers in our own time. Or equally another phrase italicized by Valéry: 'So the poet's problem must be to *draw from his practical instrument* (language) *the means to realize an essentially nonpractical work*'.

Valéry came to the conclusion that an absolute poetry was impossible—the competition with language habits and logical forms would always be too strong for it. Nevertheless the conception of an absolute poetry persisted as an ideal, and finally James Joyce came along and made it a reality.

It would be beyond the scope of this essay to trace the liberation of the word beyond Joyce, but it is to be observed that even in *Finnegans Wake* Joyce's prose remains tied to certain logical conventions. It appeals to memory, associations, word-play and punning and is therefore autocentric rather than allocentric in kind. The whole concept of a 'stream of consciousness', as William James who introduced the phrase realized, is nothing but a metaphorical convenience. Once we are 'conscious' there is no longer a stream, but an arrested image; or if there is a stream, we are only conscious of it when it has ceased to flow. When we become conscious of any *thing*, any concrete event, what we are conscious of is the sign (i.e. the word) by means of which the thing or event becomes expressible for communication. But that is precisely the difficulty, or rather the easy falsity, in communication, for the signs we habitually use are worn counters, clichés. Even to seek the true word is a step in the wrong direction, for if we consciously seek to match experience (feeling) and word, we automatically resort to the familiar cliché. Our conscious mind is a vast dictionary of clichés.

A further difficulty arises from the syntactical habit, from the habitual resort to grammatical phrases. When Mallarmé told Degas that poems were made with words not ideas, his intention was the right one, but he should not have implied that poems are 'made' (i.e. consciously composed by a *deus ex machina*, the poet). He realized well enough that the conscious poet, the poet as a personality, has to withdraw from the scene and in a very real sense let the poem write itself. What should happen, in the allo-centric perception of reality, is that the *word* should present itself, without that diminution of force that comes from declension and other syntactical drags. The word in its integrity, its uninflected thing-sound correspondence (not necessarily onomatopoeic), that alone is the poetic word.

It may be said that this sets an impossible task for the poet, but a poet is genuine to the extent that he makes use of such words: the real difficulty is for the reader, who is required to dispense with his lazy speech habits and to let the words operate freely on his sensibility. The reader must jump out of the stream and watch the words sail by, like so many bright leaves. The words become objects, objectively observed.

So long as the words can be set in the page like those gems evoked by Mallarmé's metaphor, the fire or force of the poetic afflatus can illuminate them without recourse to sustained continuity—or no more continuity than the twenty pages required for the presentation of a static poem like *Un Coup de Dés*. (The conventions of the printing press are a nuisance to the poet, as they are to a composer of music such as Boulez.) The difficulty comes when the writer's intention is narrational, as it is in the 'neo-narratives' of Arlene Zekowski and Stanley Berne. This was Joyce's difficulty, and Gertrude Stein's ; it is the difficulty of all contemporary efforts, such as those of Michel Butor *(Mobile)* or William Burroughs *(The Naked Lunch)*, to break through the blanket of grammar. It is a difficulty inherent in language, in as much as it is conceived as the *concurrent* representation of a *stream* of consciousness. The stream of consciousness is not necessarily logical, but in our attempt to reproduce it we tend to give it a grammatical structure: we introduce conjunctions and other syntactical devices which are in effect an intellectual structuring of the flowing stream.

Arlene Zekowski has suggested, very perceptively,

I

that everything will depend (for sensuous effect) on how words are received by the senses.

There has been, for a long time now, a confusion over the nature of reading literature as against reading words.

Reading literature is not a visual experience any more than painting is. It is true, in both media, we use our eyes as conductors; however, we do not think or feel with our eyes. The latter serve just as a superficial means, like petrol in a car, to activate the combustion engine into movement, so that the car will perform.

So with our eyes as merely conveyors for the combustion of experience, sensation and knowledge, which must take place within us, we read meditatively, lingering over the word or phrase packed with several levels of consciousness and association and sensuous effect.

This is all the guidance a reader needs, but it will be seen that a new discipline is demanded, as it was demanded by Mallarmé and Joyce—it is the same kind of discipline. A discipline of the senses: a tense state of awareness and apprehension. Mallarmé himself has described this state of mind ('mind' in the sense of 'set one's mind on' something):

UNE CONSTELLATION

froide d'oubli et de désuétude
        pas tant
      qu'elle n'énumère
sur quelque surface vacante et supérieure
     le heurt successif
         sidéralement
d'un compte total en formation

veillant
  doutant
    roulant
      brillant et méditant

        avant de s'arrêter
à quelque point dernier qui le sacre

The discipline required of the reader is as great as the discipline required of the writer. The lazy writer concedes too much to the lazy reader—too much in the formless form of conjunctions and prepositions. 'In art, the sentence must be destroyed because it never existed. Only words exist. And words engender thought.' But also: 'Toute Pensée émet un Coup de Dés'. Words like 'thought' and 'pensée' are misleading. What is engendered is a complex of words, an absolute of utterance; and the world still awaits, in its perfection, that Absolute.

9

AMERICAN BARDS AND BRITISH REVIEWERS

GEORGE BERNARD SHAW, in a famous quip, once described the Americans and British as two nations divided by a common language. As poets we use this common language and it is sometimes suggested, by British reviewers no less frequently than by American bards, that we use it differently. If I now proceed to throw some doubt on this belief, I do so for reasons which I hope you will not find partial. I have been asked to give a view of American poetry from abroad: my Parnassus is, however, in neutral territory where the transplanted flowers are few.

Since it is a view I am asked for, I shall begin by defining the perspective. It is a large one; it is, indeed, the perspective of world literature and to give you immediately the measure of it, let me exhibit my scale. It is one of the conveniences of history, or perhaps one of the limitations of the human vision when we look down its long perspective, that to each nation is given one towering archetypal figure, one representative poet. Greece has its Homer and Rome its Virgil; England its Shakespeare and France its Racine; Italy its Dante and Germany its Goethe. It is one of my most confident beliefs that the

United States already possesses a representative poet of this universal significance. I refer not, as might be anticipated, to Walt Whitman, but to Henry James. If you are inclined to protest that James is not a poet in the sense that Shakespeare or Dante were poets, I must beg to differ, here at the beginning of my discourse. Poetry, in this largest sense, transcends the technicalities of diction. If we who speak the English language are honest with ourselves, what does the poetry of a Greek, a Latin, a German or a French writer mean to us? We may speak a foreign language like a native, as we say; but do we, who live in another land and daily absorb other sights and sounds, hear but a distant echo of the poet's own voice? Certain languages we even designate as 'dead', so how can we, who still dispute how a vocable was uttered by an ancient poet, pretend that we are conscious of the poetic subtleties of these languages? No, in so far as our judgement of the universality of poetry rests on linguistic criteria, we must accept the verdict of the poet's own countrymen; at the same time affirming that by its very nature universality is a quality independent of locality, a question, not so much of the poet's utterance but of the width and depth of the vision or consciousness of which the living voice is but the mediating instrument.[1]

[1] How James himself felt about this question is clearly shown in a letter of 7 September 1913, to his French translator, Auguste Monod: '. . . I confess that it is a relief to me this time to have so utterly defied translation. The new volume will complete that defiance and express for me how much I feel that in a literary work of the least complexity the very form and texture are the substance itself and that the flesh is indetachable from the bones! Translation is an effort—though a

I shall presently seem to contradict this confident assertion. I do not for one moment wish to deny the verbal or vocal nature of poetry; poetry is a physical and not a metaphysical phenomenon. If we are poets we know that we not only, as Wallace Stevens said, *read* poetry with our nerves: we *write* poetry with our nerves—or, to translate the metaphor into philosophical jargon, poetry is a process of perceptual apprehension not one of a conceptual realization. But these definitions by no means exclude the works of Henry James—rather, Henry James compels us, by the very range and inclusive splendour of his perceptual apprehensions, to enlarge our conception of poetry itself. Where else, in American literature, if not in the sensitive consciousness of a Maggie Verver or Milly Theale, are we to find any such deep aesthetic awareness of the terror and beauty of the human predicament, any comparison with the poetic exercise of these powers in a Shakespeare or a Dante? In Henry James America already has a great universal poet, received, as all such poets are, with mistrust and incomprehension during his lifetime, but now at last emerging solidly into the light of universal acclaim.

Such poetry is not quotable. You may say that Shakespeare's genius is represented by certain verbal touchstones, by 'the temple-haunting martlet' or by the crow that 'makes wing to the rooky wood'. But James had his touchstones, too, though they are of

most flattering one!—to *tear* the hapless flesh, and in fact to get rid of so much of it that the living thing bleeds and faints away!' *Letters to A. C. Benson and Auguste Monod* edited by E. F. Benson. London 1930 pp 117-8

another character. I do not refer to the perfect poetic
aptness of the titles of his books—symbols that con-
dense into a concrete image the whole nature of a
tragic experience—nor to the innumerable phrases,
as isolated and as memorable as the temple-haunting martlet and the rooky wood, that overflow from
those 'full vessels of consciousness', the characters
that reflect the author's own 'lucid higher intention'. To quote such merely felicitous phrases as
touchstones of poetry would be unfaithful to what
I conceive to be the modern poet's own higher intention, which is precisely not to rely on the musical
phrase in poetic composition, but on certain larger
units which are qualities of perception—on what
James himself called, with reference to the kind of
sensibility he prized, an inordinate capacity for *being*
and *seeing*. These qualities of perception modify the
formal structure of the writing, and in this way the
style becomes idiomatic. James's own style is idiomatic in this sense—the Jamesian parenthesis, Ezra
Pound has recently suggested, *is* an American form.[1]

I won't insist further on this distinction, but will
assume that our vision has been adjusted to nearer
views of smaller objects, which is perhaps the distinctive characteristic of the modern mind. We are then
confronted with a different difficulty—the confusing
variety of what now presses on our organs of perception. Our consciousness is subjected to two pressures
which Wallace Stevens at the conclusion of his essay
on *The Noble Rider and the Sound of Words*, defined
as the reality that presses into the mind and the
imagination that presses back against the reality—'a

[1] *Paris Review* No. 28 1962 p 26

violence from within that protects us from a violence without'. Modern American poetry has been born of this clash of forces. We have to determine whether it has found a state of equilibrium poetic in its effect.

As a critic who divides his attention between poetry and painting I am apt to indulge in comparisons that do not necessarily have any logical justification. American painting (sculpture and architecture, too, but I try to simplify the situation) achieved its independence only comparatively recently, and then with a passionate conviction that threatens to exhaust itself too quickly. That independence was not a spontaneous act of revolt. Equally it was not the final ripening of a native tradition. There were some decisive historical events, accidental in their origins, such as the sojourn in the United States, under the stress of war, of foreign artists and animators like André Masson and André Breton. But, whatever the nature of the intrusive catalyst, the transformation that then took place, between the years 1940 and 1945, was complete: a new American painting emerged with its own easily recognized characteristics and was destined to revitalize the art of painting throughout the world.

In our time nothing of the same kind has happened to American poetry. The comparable poetic assault took place a hundred years ago and its 'commando' was Walt Whitman. In the interval America may have lived down Walt Whitman—their critics may have shot him in the back, but so far as the rest of the world is concerned, his soul goes marching on, and whether we are Frenchmen or Englishmen, Spaniards or Germans, we still tend to identify anything that may be distinctively American in American poetry with Whitman. And *only* with Whitman, the one pioneer as D. H. Lawrence called him. 'No English pioneers, no French. No European pioneer poets. In Europe the would-be pioneer poets are mere innovators. The same in America. Ahead of Whitman, nothing. Ahead of all poets, pioneering into the wilderness of unopened life, Whitman. Beyond him, none. His wide, strange camp at the end of the great highroad.' Lawrence wrote this in 1924 and then he could add: 'Because Whitman's camp is at the end of the road, and on the edge of a great precipice . . . there is no way down. It is a dead end'.[1]

So it has proved, in the sense intended by Lawrence. Lawrence was looking for a great leader, by which he meant a great moralist, 'a great changer of the blood in the veins of men'. But if Whitman was a dead-end it was for the very good reason that the American poets who came after him no longer responded to the forced rhetoric of the pioneer. This is not because the American poet has turned off the open road, to evade the moral issue that engaged not only Whitman, but also Hawthorne, Poe, Longfellow, Emerson and Melville; it is because the whole scene or circumstance has changed. If we cared to elaborate Lawrence's rather banal metaphor, we might say that the pioneering days being over, there is now no escaping the sophistications of a closed society, in which the road is no longer open, but winds in diminishing circles round a golden calf. The moral issue remains, inseparable from the human predicament. The best American poets are pre-

[1] From *Studies in Classic American Literature* 1924

occupied with it, but they have discovered that Whitman's rhetoric, Lawrence's too, is too brutal for the task of redemption.

After Whitman, so far as we have registered any direct impact on our transatlantic consciousness, came Ezra Pound. But Pound left America and came to Europe—came in the costume of a troubadour and when he was shamed out of it, went to school with Gautier and Remy de Gourmont, Laforgue, and Hulme. Pound, from London, served as a foreign correspondent to *Poetry*, the American review founded in Chicago fifty years ago. But the more he reported from England or France or Italy, the more evident it became that he was no longer on the road, following where Whitman had led. 'Have I a country at all?' was to be his tragic cry. 'Not that I care a curse for any nation as such or that, as far as I know, I have ever suggested that I was trying to write U.S. poetry. . . .'[1] He defected, and great poet though he be, was lost to America; and what he might have been, William Carlos Williams became. I do not mean that Dr. Williams merely stepped into some place in the ranks vacated by the poet from Idaho—I shall return to him presently. But Pound, in so far as he remained a stylistic preceptor, was as exotic and as irrelevant as Tu Fu or Fenellosa, which fact Williams realized at least as early as 1920. This is not to deny Pound's influence, even on such an indigenous poet as Williams himself. Indeed, one has only to read Pound's letters to Harriet Monroe, the founder of *Poetry*, between 1912 and 1916, to see

[1] See letter to William Carlos Williams of 11 September 1920 *Letters* pp 222, 223

how perceptively and severely he formulated the rules of the game at the decisive moment. Without his repeated insistence that poetry should be as well written as prose, that language is made out of concrete things, without his call for objectivity and concentration, for seeing and being—without this relentless campaign for purity and integrity, American poetry would never have been what it is today. Pound wrote from Europe, he had become a European, if not a Confucian; but he was preaching virtues that are universal.

At this stage in the argument it would be invidious not to make some observations on Thomas Stearns Eliot, whose roots were as authentically American as Ezra Pound's. Eliot came to England in 1914 and came to stay. He stayed to become the most universally acclaimed poet of our age—but in the becoming in what sense did he remain an American poet? Admittedly I have not yet defined what we mean by the Americanness of an American poet, but all Williams's animadversions on 'exoticism' were applied equally to Eliot as to Pound. It is perhaps an embarrassing choice for the American critic, but if he believes in the Americanness of American verse, then he must renounce Pound and Eliot, consigning them to some international limbo. He may, I think vainly, try to make some distinction between the early Eliot, the poet of *Prufrock and Other Observations* (1917) and the poet of the *Four Quartets* (1944), but the quarter of a century that intervenes is an advance from exoticism to universality, and I fail to detect anywhere, apart from the subject-matter of some of the earlier poems, any idiomatic element that could be described as specifically American. Indeed, we may conclude that Eliot's influence on the poetry of the United States has been, not only away from Whitman (not to mention Emerson and Longfellow) but towards a traditionalism altogether opposed to the American ethos and idiom.

I see that I can no longer avoid some attempt at a definition of this idiomatic element, as it strikes an observer from abroad. An idiom, any dictionary will tell us, is something one makes one's own, something peculiar to one's speech and, by extension, to the language of a people or a country. As a word it has close connections with 'idiot', but that is perhaps irrelevant. What is *not* irrelevant is that it represents a deviation from a standard, from an accepted mode of expression. The idiomatic is therefore very unclassical, and one does not expect to find idiomatic expressions in a classical language, or in a poet using a classical language. From this point of view there is certainly such a thing as a classical English language. Poets like Dryden, Gray, Tennyson and Bridges have made deliberate use of it; its use in America has been recommended by an American critic, Ivor Winters.

Classical conventions are metrical rather than verbal, systems of scansion that may be quantitative or syllabic or accentual. In this sense I do not find anything idiomatic in American verse. I know that there is a supposition, prevalent since Wordsworth first formulated it, that the diction of poetry can correspond in some close manner to the rhythms of speech and that American speech rhythms being different from British speech rhythms, the difference would constitute a new kind of poetry. But Byron, in the poem I adapted as a title for this discourse, disposed of this solecism—Wordsworth

> Who, both by precept and example, shows
> That prose is verse, and verse is merely prose;
> Convincing all, by demonstration plain,
> Poetic souls delight in prose inane. . . .

Conversational rhythms may or may not be poetic; if they are poetic the poet imitates them, not because they are conversational, but because they are exceptional. I do not wish to labour an obvious point, but in so far as we make a distinction between poetry and prose, we are making a distinction between two kinds of rhythm, a normal rhythm which is the rhythm of prose and is based on the rhythm of speech; and an abnormal rhythm which is the rhythm of poetry and is based on a heightened, an intensified, or, if you like, a regularized modification of speech rhythm. To say, with Ezra Pound, that poetry must be at least as well written as prose does not mean that it must imitate prose: it means that poetry has laws which are at least as strict as those of prose.

What I am trying to suggest, as tactfully as possible, is that the whole concept of a linguistic idiom, as distinct from a personal idiom, is an illusion. The idiom of Robert Burns, to take an extreme example, is different from the idiom of Lord Byron, but the fact that the one wrote in Scots dialect while the other wrote in King's English is poetically irrelevant.

Thou'll break my heart, thou bonnie bird
  That sings upon a bough;
Thou minds me o' the happy days
  When my fause luve was true.

Though my many faults defaced me,
  Could no other arm be found,
Than the one which once embraced me
  To inflict a cureless wound?

These two verses, the first written by Burns, the second by Byron, differ in idiom, but not in diction; but it is the diction that determines the poetry. The idiom of Donne differs from the idiom of Milton, a vast difference, but as poets they speak the same language. The difference in their speech rhythms, if it existed, was determined by physical constitution, psychological temperament, social origins and education. When Dr. Williams tells me that 'the iamb is not the normal measure of American speech' I must retort that neither is it the normal measure of British speech. When he suggests that 'the key to modern poetry is *measure*, which must reflect the flux of modern life', he is either asserting a truism, that modern poetry must suit modern tastes, or he is merely re-affirming my own contention, that the individual poet must find a measure that matches his own sensibility, his individual awareness of the visible world. But it will be *his* sensibility, *his* measure, and not one dictated by some undefined and indefinable national ethos.

When Kenneth Rexroth, interpreting William Carlos Williams, asserts that '. . . his poetic line is organically welded to American speech like muscle to bone, as the choruses of Euripides were welded to the speech of the Athenians in the market place', we are again asked to accept a truism that none of us doubts, namely, that the poet, whatever his language, must continually renew the expressive vitality of his verse by returning to what Wordsworth called 'a selection of the real language of men in a state of vivid sensation'. It is possible to maintain that the English now spoken in the United States is more 'real' in this sense than the English spoken in the East End of London or the West Riding of Yorkshire, though that remains a matter of opinion. What is not a matter of opinion, and what a British reviewer must freely acknowledge, is that the ears of the American poet are more open to these variations, these demotic phrases and expressions, than those of the majority of contemporary British poets. The comparatively greater richness in the texture of modern American poetry is no doubt explained by this closer attention to demotic speech. But have we not learned from the classic case of Wordsworth that poetry, English poetry, to the degree that it is 'classic' —I use the word again because Kenneth Rexroth calls William Carlos Williams 'the first American classic'—to that degree the poet refines the demotic ore, tempers it to some mode or measure that is essentially English?

When I examine the verse of William Carlos Williams, this first American classic, and have in my mind's eye and ear the late verse of *The Desert Music* and *Journey to Love*, I find what is in my judgement indubitably classical verse. There is a test piece which I do not insist on too strongly, for I should be using

the word 'classic' in an ambiguous sense, which is a
version from the Greek of the first Idyl of Theo-
critus.

> The whisper of the wind in
> > that pine tree,
> > > goatherd,
> is sweet as the murmur of live water;
> > likewise
> > > your flute notes. After Pan
> you shall bear away the second prize.
> > And if he
> > > take the goat
> with the horns,
> > the she-goat
> > > is yours; but if
> he choose the she-goat,
> > the kid will fall
> > > to your lot.
> And the flesh of the kid
> > is dainty
> > > before they begin milking them. . . .

What is there demotic, or American, about these
beautiful cadences? Is it not the very language of
Wyatt, of Campion, of Gray or Landor—to mention
some of the purest of our English poets? And when
we turn the pages and come to *Asphodel, That
Greeny Flower*, the poem which W. H. Auden has
rightly called 'one of the most beautiful love poems
in the language' (he did not say 'in the American
language') we find verse of such pellucid brightness,
of such simple human and passionate sentiment, that
no sense of time and place ever obtrudes between
the ear and the music, between the poet and his

audience. This is universal poetry and the language is English.

I must admit a personal predilection for the poetry of William Carlos Williams. It may be that American in the grain as he is, and English as I am (in this context I refuse to call myself British), we share the same idiosyncrasies. But any critic's point of view, if he be honest, is determined by physical facts, by constitutional elements that are also responsible for the psychological facts. The voice of the poet has the timbre of his body and that, as I have already suggested, is the only sense in which we should use the word 'idiom'. But if, in our examination of contemporary American poetry, we are thrown back on the psychological facts, what then do we find?

We find certain poets who, from a distant view, are typically American. We find Hart Crane, Wallace Stevens, Robert Lowell and John Berryman, the American poets currently most admired and imitated by the younger British poets. Have these four anything in common that is distinctively American? Having rejected the claim to an exclusively American idiom, can we perhaps admit in its place an exclusively American psyche?

Waldo Frank has said that the poetry of Hart Crane is 'a deliberate continuance of the great tradition in terms of our industrialized world'—the great tradition that 'rose in the Mediterranean world with the will of Egypt, Israel and Greece, to recreate the individual and the group in the image of values called divine'. Crane himself, in his short but highly significant essay, *Modern Poetry*, affirmed that the function of poetry in a Machine Age is identical with

K

its function in any other age; and that 'its capacities
for presenting the most complete synthesis of human
values remain essentially immune from any of the so-
called inroads of science'. The point is not that
poetry should absorb the machine, but that it should
'*acclimatize* it as naturally and casually as trees,
cattle, galleons, castles and all other human associations of the past. . . .' Otherwise poetry 'has failed of
its contemporary function'. Those who go to Hart
Crane for a justification of an American idiom will
be disappointed. They will find instead a traditionalist, his verse grounded on the practice of early
English prosody, in some sense specifically Elizabethan, a traditionalist aware that (to quote his own
words) 'the most intense and eloquent current verse
derives sheerly from acute psychological analysis,
quite independent of any dramatic motivation'.

There you have the description, if not the definition, of the quality most distinctively American in
American verse, the revealed tension between
analysis and motivation, reality and imagination; and
it is highly significant that Crane himself found the
source of this quality in Whitman—'The most typical
and valid expression of the American *psychosis*
seems to me still to be found in Whitman', he wrote
in this same essay. 'He, better than any other, was
able to co-ordinate those forces in America which
seem most intractable, fusing them into a universal
vision which takes on additional significance as time
goes on.' Earlier in the essay he had quoted Coleridge's definition of genius as 'the power of acting
creatively under laws of its own origination', and
he concludes that Whitman was a revolutionist be-

yond the strict meaning of this definition, 'but his bequest is still to be realized in all its implications'.

A British reviewer may therefore suggest, not only that Crane himself did his best to realize Whitman's bequest, but also that what is distinctive in American poetry since Crane's death has been a continuation of this attempt to find a valid expression of the American psychosis. Before I ask for agreement I must, of course, make some attempt of my own to define the American psychosis, or rather, to make a significant choice among the many diagnoses of this psychosis made by American critics and psychologists. Richard Blackmur once reproved Crane for using this word 'psychosis' and both he and Professor Winters have a poor opinion of Crane's transcendentalism. But somehow Crane survives their criticisms. We remember Dr. Williams's protest, that 'it isn't what (a man) *says* that counts as a work of art, it's what he makes, with such intensity of perception that it lives with an intrinsic movement of its own to verify its authenticity'. Words that remind me incidentally of one of Henry James's definitions of lyric poetry—'stony-hearted triumphs of objective form'.

Critics, alas, cannot do without a philosophic sounding-board: it is the only thing that makes us resound at all, for in the physical presence of the poem, or the picture, we can but register our sensations. The great intelligence—yes, that too is necessary; but it is a crudity of sensibility to imagine that the poet's or the painter's intelligence functions as an acceptable philosophy. What philosophy did a great painter like Turner profess? For that matter, what philosophy did our greatest poet profess? Some critics have tried to derive a philosophy from Shakespeare's works, but they have only succeeded in revealing a great confusion.

I think we should respect Crane's brief excursion into the definition of modern poetry because even if it does not measure up to the logician's standards of consistency or profundity, it does indicate the poet's own intention more nearly than any critical analysis from the outside. His use of the word 'psychosis' may not be clinically correct, but Crane obviously thought that it was adequate to describe the alienation caused by the machine, and the title of his greatest poem *The Bridge* was chosen deliberately as a psychological symbol.

But what separate shores was this symbolic Bridge meant to connect? The last section of the poem is entitled *Atlantis* and it is headed by a quotation from Plato: 'Music is then the knowledge of that which relates to love in harmony and form'. Substitute, without any violence to Plato's meaning, the word 'poetry' for 'music' and Crane's message becomes clear:

O Thou steeled Cognizance whose leap commits
The agile precincts of the lark's return;
Within whose lariat sweep encinctured sing
In single chrysalis the many twain,—
Of stars thou art the stitch and stallionglow
And like an organ, Thou, with sound of doom—
Sight, sound and flesh Thou leadest from time's realm
As love strikes clear direction for the helm.

The Bridge, by connecting imagination and reality, heals the dichotomy in man's mind—the mind can then advance along Whitman's Open Road, and that is precisely what Crane affirms, in that section of his poem called *Cape Hatteras*, where the 'joyous seer' is invoked by name and where

> Vast engines outward veering with seraphic grace
> On clarion cylinders pass out of sight
> To course that span of consciousness[1] thou'st named
> The Open Road—thy vision is reclaimed!

Crane, like James, had a complete and consistent awareness of a particular world of appearances, the world of Manhattan, of subways and sidewalks, of derricks and cables, of docks and piers, of the sleepless river and the encircling sea; of the 'lovely and herded men' lost in this inorganic wilderness, this waste land. There is no poet of London, or indeed of Paris or Rome or any other great city (unless it is

[1] With the word 'consciousness' we return to Henry James and his conception of the poet's function, what he called the generality and comprehensiveness of the poet's impulse. James, according to Dr. Dorothea Krook believed 'that art concerns itself to render the world of appearances; that these appearances exist only in the consciousness, indeed, *are* the content of the consciousness, of human observers; that the world of art therefore is a beautiful representation of the appearances present to a particular consciousness under particular conditions, and the artist's overriding task is accordingly to exhibit in the concrete, with the greatest possible completeness and consistency, as well as vividness and intensity, the particular world of appearances accessible to a particular consciousness under the specific conditions created for it by the artist' . . . In this wider consciousness any distinction between the poet and the novelist disappears, as I said at the beginning of this lecture. Any definition of artistic consciousness, as James himself said, 'makes but a mouthful of so minor a distinction, in the fields of light, as that between verse and prose'. *The Ordeal of Consciousness in Henry James*. Cambridge University Press 1962 p 399

Bert Brecht of Berlin) who has had such a comprehensive vision—again a vision and not a theory—of our specifically modern predicament, that is to say, of our alienation. If the poetry of the American psychosis had been carried no further, it would, in Crane's work, remain a unique achievement in contemporary poetry. But Crane was to be followed by other poets, distinctively American in their concern for acute 'psychological analysis'.

At this point I would like to remind you once more that I am trying to present to you, not a personal point of view, but that of British poets who speak the same language as American poets. My own vision is slightly myopic—I do not see very clearly beyond the poets of my own generation—Pound, Eliot, Williams, Crane, Tate and Marianne Moore. These are not the poets who most excite the younger generation in Great Britain. Wallace Stevens is an exception because, owing to the accidents of publication, his work has had a delayed action. I suspect that what appeals to our younger poets—disciples for the most part of Professor Empson—is the sophistication of Stevens's work—an aspect of his work that has also attracted the younger poets of America. Our young poets praise Stevens as 'a great master of lyrical meditation'—I quote from their reviews—as 'one of the most considerable poets of the last hundred years', 'one of the major poets of this century'—no other American poet has earned such hyperboles.

Stevens said many apparently contradictory things about poetry, and about his own poetry in particular (perhaps to keep pace with the changing nature of that poetry) but on one point he was firm—in his own words—'the artist, the presence of the determining personality. Without that reality no amount of other things matter much'. His ideal artist was a painter, Cézanne, one who knew better than any of his contemporaries how to resist 'the pressure of external event or events on the consciousness to the exclusion of any power of contemplation'. The poetry of Stevens may be interpreted as, in this sense, a triumphant exclusion of the American scene— though not necessarily of what Crane called the American psychosis, which I am inclined to believe is not American at all. The alienation that causes this psychosis is a condition of man everywhere in our technological civilization.

It is a question, therefore, of creating a life of the imagination at least as forceful as the reality of the machine—the 'harde iron' of a poem by Marianne Moore, on which Stevens wrote a commentary, contrasting the mythical bird of Miss Moore's imagination with the real ostrich of the Encyclopaedia Britannica—the achieved or individual reality emerging as more potent than the bird of the ornithologist. Cézanne never painted an ostrich, and if he had done so, it would not have borne much resemblance to the ostrich in Miss Moore's poem. Cézanne strove to realize his sensations in front of nature. It was an effort of the imagination, but the images involved were given in contemplation: they were a penetration and correction of visual habits, perceptual conventions. But according to Stevens—and I believe he is accurately describing his own and perhaps Miss Moore's intention—the poem is what he calls a 'transcendent analogue' of the reality revealed to our perceptions. Reality is broken down into particulars in order that these particulars may be reassembled according to the heart's desire, the heart being, in Steven's anatomy, an organ of 'affabulation'. I am not questioning this analysis of the poetic process—on the contrary, I agree that 'the venerable, the fundamental books of the human spirit are vast collections of such analogues'. But what have these analogues to do with the American scene, or the American idiom; what, indeed, have they to do with the American psychosis, except as abstract symbols of its complexity?

Stevens often refers to painters like Watteau and Fragonard as though he had a special sympathy for their charming, artificial fantasies. I believe that his own poetry, by intention, belongs to the same elegant tradition, with whimsicalities and satirical quirks for which Callot or Goya would be a more appropriate comparison. The habit of contemplation which he cultivated gradually led to a dulling of his 'perceptual apprehensions'; the analogues became metaphysically transcendent. But the metaphysics was no longer poetry; as Cowley was no longer Donne.

An American critic, Randall Jarrell, once pointed out that Stevens had the weakness—'a terrible one for a poet'—of thinking of particulars as primarily illustrations of general truths, which is the inverse of the poetic process, which always requires the poet 'to treat the concrete as primary'.[1] Stevens antici-

[1] Randall Jarrell *Poetry and the Age* Faber & Faber London 1955 p 130

pated the criticism, denying that 'abstraction is a vice except To the fatuous'. Mr. Jarrell had Goethe's saying in mind, that 'it makes a great difference whether the poet seeks the particular in relation to the universal or contemplates the universal in the particular. . . . (In the first case) the particular functions as an example, as an instance of the universal; but the second indeed represents the very nature of poetry. He who grasps this particular as living essence also encompasses the universal'. One of our British reviewers, and a very competent one, Frank Kermode, has dealt very effectively with Mr. Jarrell's objection, affirming that there is, Goethe's saying not withstanding, such a thing as a poetry of the abstract.[1] Order itself, the enduring form if not the living essence of any art, is itself an abstraction. It is the ambiguity of the word 'abstract' that confuses this discussion; abstraction is always interpreted as abstraction from particulars; conceptualization is the vice.

Goethe's text, used by Mr. Jarrell to reveal a possible weakness in Stevens, might serve equally well to indicate the strength of Robert Lowell. His poetry from its beginnings was always a poetry of particulars, of bright particular images, in which the poet encompasses the universals of our human destiny. In his poetry the minute particular, the 'terrible crystal' of Richard Watson Dixon, serves as the precipitative agent. The whole of the Lowell family, very particular people, their heirlooms and their habits, are sacrificed on this demanding altar of the universal. It is such sacrifices, efficiently per-

[1] Frank Kermode *Wallace Stevens* Oliver & Boyd, Edinburgh and London 1960

formed, that inspire reverence. But Lowell is no innovator—least of all American poets can he be cast for the role of indigenous bard. His masters are European—Villon and Baudelaire, Rimbaud and Rilke. The texture of his verse is traditional and reaches back perhaps fifty years for its historical links. Do I exaggerate? Let me try an experiment. I shall quote two passages, one from Robert Lowell's narrative poem *The Mills of the Kavanaughs*, the other from a poem first published in London in 1913. You may, or you may not, detect the transition from one to the other:

> So gazing, like one stunned, it reached his mind
> That the hedge brambles overhung the brook
> More than was right, making the selvage blind
> The dragging brambles too much flotsam took.
> Dully he thought to mend. He fetched a hook,
> And standing in the shallow stream he slashed,
> For hours, it seemed; the thorns, the twigs, the dead
>   leaves splashed,
> Splashed and were bobbed away across the shallows;
> Pale grasses with the sap gone from them fell,
> Sank, or were carried down beyond the sallows.
> The bruised ground-ivy gave out earthy-smell. . . .
> And now the mussed blue-bottles bead her float:
> Bringers of luck. Of luck? At worst, a rest
> From counting blisters on her metal boat,
> That spins and staggers. North and south and west:
> A scene, perhaps, of Fragonard—her park,
> Whose planted poplars scatter penny-leaves,
> White underneath, like mussels to the dark
> Chop of the shallows.

There is perhaps more individuality in the last eight lines, which are Lowell's, but in tone and cadence, in image and atmosphere, they seem to form an organic continuity with the other lines, which come from *The Daffodil Fields* of John Masefield. But while I was quoting these lines from Masefield's forgotten poem I was conscious also of the voice of Robert Frost; and where, indeed, in distilling the essence, shall we find any difference of accent or cadence, of measure or idiom, between the poetry of Masefield, Housman, Hardy or Edward Thomas and American poets so essentially post—or anti—modernist (again I borrow a judgement from Mr. Jarrell) as Robert Lowell—or, to make a balance of names, John Berryman, Richard Wilbur, Delmore Schwartz and Randall Jarrell himself?

To describe Lowell as post- or anti-modernist is not to make a qualitative judgement. To deserve to be ranked with Hardy or even with Masefield (a poet unduly neglected by British critics) is no mean achievement. But it does not, of course, bring out the distinctive quality in Lowell's verse which, to adopt a phrase from Wallace Stevens, is a violence from within that seems to accept, as punishment, the violence from without. The masochism has, I believe, been noted before. There is no artifice here, no 'trancendent analogue', but rather a resentment too bitter for disguise:

> I walk upon the flood:
> My way is wayward; there is no way out:
> Now how the weary waters swell,—
> The tree is down in blood!
> All the bats of Babel flap about
> The rising sun of hell.

Violence it is, that almost overwhelms the poetry with its passionate excess. The same tendency is revealed in Robert Lowell's choice of models, 'the dark and against the grain', as he calls them in his recent *Imitations*. I doubt if full justice has been done to this volume—certainly not by British reviewers. Forget for a moment that these poems are derivative in conception—that another poet in another language invented the occasion, found the image and the idea. Then consider Lowell's claim, that nothing like these poems 'exists in English, for the excellence of a poet depends on the unique opportunities of his native language', and if you admit this, as I think you must, then I think you must admit the thesis I have ventured to put before you—that whatever its origin, whatever its occasion, English poetry is English, and that as American or British poets (Australian or Canadian) we seize the opportunities of a unique language and succeed in creating a poetry to the extent that we exploit the singular music and expressiveness of that language.

Music *and* expressiveness—I use these words as if they were inevitable aspects of the same poetic reality, but it may be that the distinctive achievement of modern poetry is to have separated them and to have made expressiveness the single criterion. Once again I would call attention to the parallel to be found in the plastic arts. There, in the past eighty or hundred years, a distinct style has been developed to which we give the name of expressionism and the exponents of this style have quite deliberately renounced the ideal of beauty, which ever since the great age of Greek sculpture had been the universally accepted ideal of humanist art, and have substituted the ideal of *vitality*. 'Beauty, in the later Greek or Renaissance sense, is not the aim of my sculpture,' is the affirmation of one of our greatest contemporary artists, Henry Moore: 'for me a work must first have a vitality of its own'. The music or the measure of words, the modern poet seems to say, is not the aim of my verse; for me a poem must first have an intensity of its own. It would be difficult to find anywhere in the verses we have been discussing single lines or images to match Matthew Arnold's mauled touchstones, or even Allen Tate's brighter list. The modern poet seems to lack the very ambition to write of 'bare ruined choirs, where late the sweet birds sang'; such music is too sweet for his psychological muse. Instead he will show us 'a mother skunk with her column of kittens swill(ing) the garbage pail'.

I have spent so much effort in the past trying to justify expressionism in painting and sculpture to have the inconsistent desire to attack it in poetry. When a British reviewer praises American poets for 'coping openly with the quick of their experience, experience sometimes on the edge of disintegration and breakdown',[1] I recognize that he is praising poets for qualities for which, in the past, I have praised painters and sculptors. But to praise Munch or Van Gogh, Kokoschka or Beckmann, has not led me to renounce Cézanne or Matisse, Bonnard or Chagall. Though beauty and vitality have been separate ideals in the plastic arts, they still preserve a certain

[1] *The New Poetry*. Selected and edited by A. Alvarez. Penguin Books 1962

equilibrium in the total achievement. I am not sure that in poetry, despite the touchstones to be found in an Eliot or a Frost, we can now make the same claim. The British reviewer I have just quoted, Mr. Alvarez, proudly asserts that modern poets have gone 'beyond the Gentility Principle'. It is possible, of course, that he is confusing gentility and grace.

It would seem that I am about to conclude with a defence of pure poetry. It is true that in the plastic arts my preference is given to the representation of pure form, to the kind of art we call 'abstract'. I agree with that great poet Mistral, whom Paul Valéry so greatly respected, that 'form alone exists—only form preserves the works of the mind'. I think Wallace Stevens meant the same by 'the idea of order', the 'blessed rage for order'. I admit that poetry is a formal aspect of language—that English poetry is the most expressive order of our English tongue. But what gives it vitality and beauty, in indissoluble unity, is a spiritual resonance proceeding from the organic substance and structure of our speech. American poetry in our time, indeed ever since the time of Whitman, has been a great poetry because it has renewed the spiritual vitality of the English language—'made it new' as certain Irish writers—Shaw and Yeats—also in their time made it new. In an essay on *The Argentine Writer and Tradition*, Jorge Borges, whose argument in respect of the Spanish poet in our time is the same as mine in respect of the English poet, reminds us that Gibbon in his *Decline and Fall of the Roman Empire*, observes that in the Arabian book *par excellence*, in the Koran, there are no camels; and Borges believes 'that if there were any doubt as to the authenticity of the Koran, this absence of camels would be sufficient to prove it as an Arabian work. It was written by Mohammed, and Mohammed, as an Arab, has no reason to know that camels were especially Arabian; for him they were part of reality, he has no reason to emphasize them; on the other hand, the first thing a falsifier, a tourist, an Arab nationalist would do is to have a surfeit of camels, caravans of camels on every page; but Mohammed, as an Arab, was unconcerned; he knew he could be an Arab without camels'. In the same way, and for the same reason, I believe that a poet can be an American without mentioning whatever you may choose as the American camel—perhaps Mr. Lowell's mother skunk.

The English language, the physical substance from which our poetry has been smelted, the linguistic ore of our eloquence, the formative matrix of our consciousness, of our imagery, of our intelligence, is greater than the demotic idiom of any of the numerous peoples that now speak this language. We often refer to the pure well of English undefil'd, but the well-worn metaphor is too static. My revision of it will be equally banal, but we might say that English was formed from many remote linguistic sources which as they gained force and definition became associated with personal names—Chaucer, Wyclif, Malory; Wyatt, Surrey, Skelton; Drayton, Daniel, Sidney—sources that met and became bright mountain becks and winding streams, that in Spenser and Marlowe are already headlong torrents soon to unite in the wide and irresistible river that flows on from Shakespeare and Milton. In that current we still have our only existence.

I have, I hope, made my meaning clear. As poets we do but diminish our stature and strength if we claim to steer a separate course. To be an English poet is a great honour, the greatest honour that is given to a poet and the envy of the poets of the whole world. We have most dignity, whatever our origins, if we acknowledge the long and vital tradition of our common language and strive, not to speak with a wayward accent, but as purely as our individual sensibility will allow. That, I believe, is what the best American poets have done. Their achievement is to have approached, more nearly than their British contemporaries, the grace, the realism and the intensity that were always the proper virtues of an English verse.